Python for Data Science: A Practical Approach to Machine Learning

JARREL E.

Contents

Acknowledgment

I extend my sincere gratitude to the individuals and resources that have played a pivotal role in the creation of this book. Their expertise, guidance, and support have been invaluable throughout this journey.

Thank you for sharing your deep insights into the intricate world of Python, data science, and machine learning. Your technical expertise has been instrumental in shaping the content of this book.

I appreciate the thorough review and constructive feedback provided by the reviewers. Your meticulous examination has undoubtedly enhanced the quality and accuracy of the material.

Data Science Community: I extend my gratitude to the vibrant and dynamic data science community for its continuous inspiration. The collective knowledge and passion within the community have been a driving force behind the practical insights shared in this book.

Family and Friends: To my family and friends who provided unwavering support, understanding, and encouragement, I am profoundly grateful. Your belief in this project has been a constant motivation.

Readers: Last but not least, to the readers who embark on this learning journey – your curiosity and commitment to mastering Python for data science and machine learning are the fuel that propels the impact of this book.

This collaborative effort reflects the dedication of a community passionate about advancing the field of data science. Thank you to each contributor for being an integral part of "Python for Data Science: A Practical Approach to Machine Learning."

Forward

This book is a comprehensive journey into the heart of data manipulation, analysis, and the application of machine learning algorithms using the Python programming language. Its purpose is to equip both beginners and seasoned practitioners with the tools and knowledge needed to navigate the complexities of this dynamic field.

Navigating the Python Landscape: The book begins by laying a solid foundation in Python, ensuring that readers, regardless of their programming background, can confidently navigate the language's syntax and data structures. With clarity and precision, it demystifies the intricacies of Python, making it an accessible and powerful tool for data analysis.

Unveiling the World of Data Science: From there, the exploration delves into the fundamental principles of data science. Readers will find a comprehensive guide to data cleaning, exploration, and visualization, laying the groundwork for informed decision-making. The book's practical approach ensures that theoretical concepts are immediately applied, reinforcing learning through hands-on examples and exercises.

Machine Learning in Action: The heart of the book lies in its coverage of machine learning. From the basics of supervised and unsupervised learning to the intricacies of deep learning, each concept is presented in a practical, real-world context. Through clear explanations and illustrative examples, readers will not only understand the theoretical underpinnings but also gain the skills to implement and experiment with machine learning algorithms.

Real-world Applications: In the final sections, the book goes beyond the theoretical realm, providing insights into the practical applications of Python in data science. Case studies and real-world examples illustrate how Python can be employed to solve complex problems, empowering readers to confidently apply their knowledge in diverse scenarios.

A Call to Action: As we traverse the pages of Python for Data Science: A Practical Approach to Machine Learning, my hope is that readers not only acquire a set of skills but also develop a mindset—a mindset that sees challenges as opportunities, that views data as a narrative waiting to be told, and that recognizes Python as the enabler of these narratives.

Preface

In the pulsating realm of data science, Python has emerged not just as a programming language but as a powerful ally, empowering data enthusiasts to unravel the mysteries concealed within vast datasets. As I present "Python for Data Science: A Practical Approach to Machine Learning," my aim is to guide you through this dynamic landscape, providing a hands-on and comprehensive exploration of Python's applications in the realm of data science and machine learning.

This book is designed for both novices venturing into the world of data science and seasoned practitioners seeking a practical guide to harnessing Python's potential. The journey begins with a solid foundation in Python programming, ensuring that readers of all backgrounds can embark on this expedition with confidence.

We then delve into the core principles of data science, unraveling the intricacies of data manipulation, exploration, and visualization. The emphasis is not just on theory but on immediate application. Through step-by-step examples and exercises, you will gain the skills to wrangle data and extract meaningful insights.

The heart of the book lies in its exploration of machine learning. From understanding the basics to implementing complex algorithms, each chapter is crafted to provide a blend of theoretical understanding and practical application. Whether you are new to machine learning or seeking to deepen your knowledge, this book offers a road map to navigate this fascinating landscape.

Basics

We are living in the 'age of data' that is enriched with better computational power and more storage resources,. This data or information is increasing day by day, but the real challenge is to make sense of all the data. Businesses & organizations are trying to deal with it by building intelligent systems using the concepts and methodologies from Data science, Data Mining and Machine learning. Among them, machine learning is the most exciting field of computer science. It would not be wrong if we call machine learning the application and science of algorithms that provides sense to the data.

What is Machine Learning?

Machine Learning (ML)is that field of computer science with the help of which computer systems can provide sense to data in much the same way as human beings do.

In simple words, ML is a type of artificial intelligence that extract patterns out of raw data by using an algorithm or method. The main focus of ML is to allow computer systems learn from experience without being explicitly programmed or human intervention.

Need for Machine Learning

Human beings, at this moment, are the most intelligent and advanced species on earth because they can think, evaluate and solve complex problems. On the other side, AI is still in it's initial stage and haven't surpassed human intelligence in many aspects. Then the question is that what is the need to make machine learn? The most suitable reason for doing this is, "to make decisions, based on data, with efficiency and scale".

Lately, organizations are investing heavily in newer technologies like Artificial Intelligence, Machine Learning and Deep Learning to get the key information from data to perform several real-world tasks and solve problems. We can call it data-driven decisions taken by machines, particularly to automate the process. These data-driven decisions can be used, instead of using programming logic, in the problems that cannot be programmed inherently. The fact is that we can't do without human intelligence, but other aspect is that we all need to solve real-world problems with efficiency at a huge scale. That is why the need for machine learning arises.

Why & When to Make Machines Learn?

We have already discussed the need for machine learning, but another question arises that in what scenarios we must make the machine learn? There can be several circumstances where we need machines to take data-driven decisions with efficiency and at a huge scale. The followings are some of such circumstances where making machines learn would be more effective:

Lack of human expertise

The very first scenario in which we want a machine to learn and take data-driven decisions, can be the domain where there is a lack of human expertise. The examples can be navigation in unknown territories or spatial planets.

Dynamic scenarios

There are some scenarios which are dynamic in nature i.e. they keep changing over time. In case of these scenarios and behaviors, we want a machine to learn and take data-driven decisions. Some of the examples can be network connectivity and availability of infrastructure in an organization.

Difficulty in translating expertise into computational tasks

There can be various domains in which humans have their expertise,; however, they are unable to translate this expertise into computational tasks. In such circumstances we want machine learning. The examples can be the domains of speech recognition, cognitive tasks etc.

Machine Learning Model

Before discussing the machine learning model, we must need to understand the following formal definition of ML given by professor Mitchell:

"A computer program is said to learn from experience E with respect to some class of tasks T and performance measure P, if its performance at tasks in T, as measured by P, improves with experience E."

The above definition is basically focusing on three parameters, also the main components of any learning algorithm, namely Task(T), Performance(P) and experience (E). In this context, we can simplify this definition as:

ML is a field of AI consisting of learning algorithms that:

- Improve their performance (P)
- At executing some task (T)
- Over time with experience (E)

Based on the above, the following diagram represents a Machine Learning Model:

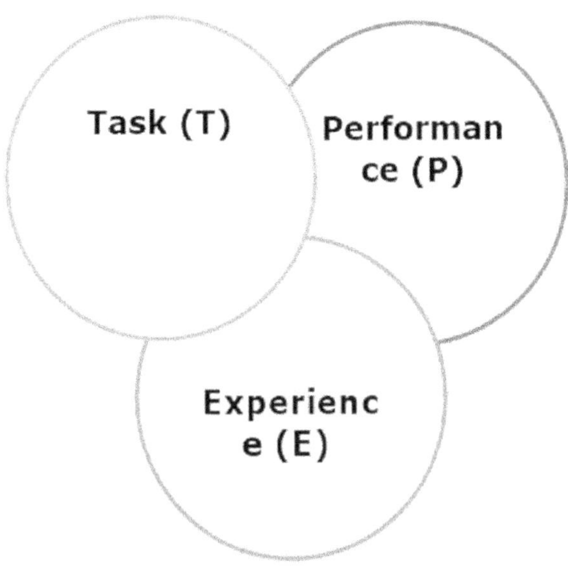

Let us discuss them more in detail now:

Task(T)

From the perspective of problem, we may define the task T as the real-world problem to be solved. The problem can be anything like finding best house price in a specific location or to find best marketing strategy etc. On the other hand, if we talk about machine learning, the definition of task is different because it is difficult to solve ML based tasks by conventional programming approach.

A task T is said to be a ML based task when it is based on the process and the system must follow for operating on data points. The examples of ML based tasks are Classification, Regression, Structured annotation, Clustering, Transcription etc.

Experience (E)

As name suggests, it is the knowledge gained from data points provided to the algorithm or model. Once provided with the dataset, the model will run iteratively and will learn some inherent pattern. The learning thus acquired is called experience(E). Making an analogy with human learning, we can think of this situation as in which a human being is learning or gaining some experience from various attributes like situation, relationships etc. Supervised, unsupervised and reinforcement learning are some ways to learn or gain experience. The experience gained by out ML model or algorithm will be used to solve the task T.

Performance (P)

An ML algorithm is supposed to perform task and gain experience with the passage of time. The measure which tells whether ML algorithm is performing as per expectation or not is its performance (P). P is basically a quantitative metric that tells how a model is performing the task, T, using its experience, E. There are many metrics that help to understand the ML performance, such as accuracy score, F1 score, confusion matrix, precision, recall, sensitivity etc.

Challenges in Machines Learning

While Machine Learning is rapidly evolving, making significant strides with cyber security and autonomous cars, this segment of AI as whole still has a long way to go. The reason behind is that ML has not been able to overcome number of challenges. The challenges that ML is facing currently are:

Quality of data: Having good-quality data for ML algorithms is one of the biggest challenges. Use of low-quality data leads to the problems related to data preprocessing and feature extraction.

Time-Consuming task: Another challenge faced by ML models is the consumption of time especially for data acquisition, feature extraction and retrieval.

Lack of specialist persons: As ML technology is still in its infancy stage, availability of expert resources is a tough job.

No clear objective for formulating business problems: Having no clear objective and well-defined goal for business problems is another key challenge for ML because this technology is not that mature yet.

Issue of overfitting & underfitting: If the model is overfitting or underfitting, it cannot be represented well for the problem.

Curse of dimensionality: Another challenge ML model faces is too many features of data points. This can be a real hindrance.

Difficulty in deployment: Complexity of the ML model makes it quite difficult to be deployed in real life.

Applications of Machines Learning

Machine Learning is the most rapidly growing technology and according to researchers we are in the golden year of AI and ML. It is used to solve many real-world complex problems which cannot be solved with traditional approach. Following are some real-world applications of ML:

- Emotion analysis
- Sentiment analysis
- Error detection and prevention
- Weather forecasting and prediction
- Stock market analysis and forecasting
- Speech synthesis
- Speech recognition
- Customer segmentation
- Object recognition
- Fraud detection
- Fraud prevention
- Recommendation of products to customer in online shopping.

Python Ecosystem

An Introduction to Python

Python is a popular object-oriented programming language having the capabilities of high- level programming language. Its easy to learn syntax and portability capability makes it popular these days. The followings facts gives us the introduction to Python:

- Python was developed by Guido van Rossum at Stichting Mathematisch Centrum in the Netherlands.
- It was written as the successor of programming language named 'ABC'.
- It's first version was released in 1991.
- The name Python was picked by Guido van Rossum from a TV show named Monty Python's Flying Circus.
- It is an open source programming language which means that we can freely download it and use it to develop programs. It can be downloaded from www.python.org.
- Python programming language is having the features of Java and C both. It is having the elegant 'C' code and on the other hand, it is having classes and objects like Java for object-oriented programming.

- It is an interpreted language, which means the source code of Python program would be first converted into bytecode and then executed by Python virtual machine.

Strengths and Weaknesses of Python

Every programming language has some strengths as well as weaknesses, so does Python too.

Strengths

According to studies and surveys, Python is the fifth most important language as well as the most popular language for machine learning and data science. It is because of the following strengths that Python has:

Easy to learn and understand: The syntax of Python is simpler; hence it is relatively easy, even for beginners also, to learn and understand the language.

Multi-purpose language: Python is a multi-purpose programming language because it supports structured programming, object-oriented programming as well as functional programming.

Huge number of modules: Python has huge number of modules for covering every aspect of programming. These modules are easily available for use hence making Python an extensible language.

Support of open source community: As being open source

programming language, Python is supported by a very large developer community. Due to this, the bugs are easily fixed by the Python community. This characteristic makes Python very robust and adaptive.

Scalability: Python is a scalable programming language because it provides an improved structure for supporting large programs than shell-scripts.

Weakness

Although Python is a popular and powerful programming language, it has its own weakness of slow execution speed.

The execution speed of Python is slow as compared to compiled languages because Python is an interpreted language. This can be the major area of improvement for Python community.

Installing Python

For working in Python, we must first have to install it. You can perform the installation of Python in any of the following two ways:

- Installing Python individually
- Using Pre-packaged Python distribution: Anaconda

Let us discuss these each in detail.

Installing Python Individually

If you want to install Python on your computer, then then you need to download only the binary code applicable for your platform. Python distribution is available for Windows, Linux and Mac platforms.

The following is a quick overview of installing Python on the above-mentioned platforms:

On Unix and Linux platform

With the help of following steps, we can install Python on Unix and Linux platform:

- First, go to https://www.python.org/downloads/.
- Next, click on the link to download zipped source code available for Unix/Linux.
- Now, Download and extract files.
- Next, we can edit the *Modules/Setup* file if we want to customize some options.
- Next, write the command **run ./configure script** make install

On Windows platform

With the help of following steps, we can install Python on Windows platform:

- First, go to https://www.python.org/downloads/.
- Next, click on the link for Windows installer *python-XYZ.msi* file. Here XYZ is the version we wish to install.
- Now, we must run the file that is downloaded. It will take

us to the Python install wizard, which is easy to use. Now, accept the default settings and wait until the install is finished.

On Macintosh platform

For Mac OS X, Homebrew, a great and easy to use package installer is recommended to install Python 3. In case if you don't have Homebrew, you can install it with the help of following command:

```
$ ruby -e "$(curl -fsSL
https://raw.githubusercontent.com/Homebrew/install/master/insta
```

It can be updated with the command below:

```
$ brew update
```

Now, to install Python3 on your system, we need to run the following command:

```
$ brew install python3
```

Using Pre-packaged Python Distribution: Anaconda

Anaconda is a packaged compilation of Python which have all the libraries widely used in Data science. We can follow the following steps to setup Python environment using Anaconda:

Step 1: First, we need to download the required installation package from Anaconda distribution. The link for the same is https://www.anaconda.com/distribution/. You can choose from Windows, Mac and Linux OS as per your requirement.

Step 2: Next, select the Python version you want to install on your machine. The latest Python version is 3.7.There you will get the options for 64-bit and 32-bit Graphical installer both.

Step 3: After selecting the OS and Python version, it will download the Anaconda installer on your computer. Now, double click the file and the installer will install Anaconda package.

Step 4: For checking whether it is installed or not, open a command prompt and type Python as follows:

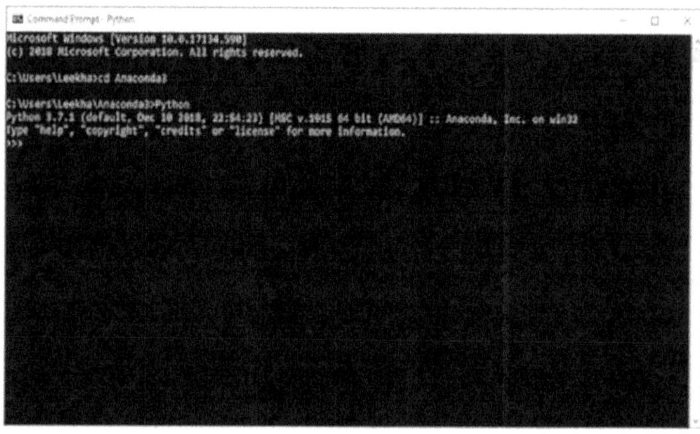

Why Python for Data Science?

Python is the fifth most important language as well as most popular language for Machine learning and data science. The following are the features of Python that makes it the preferred choice of language for data science:

Extensive set of packages

Python has an extensive and powerful set of packages which are ready to be used in various domains. It also has packages like **numpy, scipy, pandas, scikit-learn** etc. which are required for machine learning and data science.

Easy prototyping

Another important feature of Python that makes it the choice of language for data science is the easy and fast prototyping. This feature is useful for developing new algorithm.

Collaboration feature

The field of data science basically needs good collaboration and Python provides many useful tools that make this extremely.

One language for many domains

A typical data science project includes various domains like data extraction, data manipulation, data analysis, feature extraction, modeling, evaluation, deployment and updating the solution. As Python is a multi-purpose language, it allows the data scientist to address all these domains from a common platform.

Components of Python ML Ecosystem

In this section, let us discuss some core Data Science libraries that form the components of Python Machine learning ecosystem. These useful components make modeling important language for Data Science. Though there are many such components, let us discuss some of the importance components of Python ecosystem here:

Jupyter Notebook

Jupyter notebooks basically provides an interactive computational environment for developing Python based Data Science applications. They are formerly known as ipython notebooks. The following are some of the features of Jupyter notebooks that makes it one of the best components of Python ML ecosystem:

- Jupyter notebooks can illustrate the analysis process step by step by arranging the stuff like code, images, text, output etc. in a step by step manner.
- It helps a data scientist to document the thought process while developing the analysis process.
- One can also capture the result as the part of the notebook.
- With the help of jupyter notebooks, we can share our work with a peer also.

Installation and Execution

If you are using Anaconda distribution, then you need not install jupyter notebook separately as it is already installed with it. You just need to go to Anaconda Prompt and type the following command:

```
C:\>jupyter notebook
```

After pressing enter, it will start a notebook server at local-host:8888 of your computer. It is shown in the following screen shot:

Now, after clicking the New tab, you will get a list of options. Select Python 3 and it will take you to the new notebook for start working in it. You will get a glimpse of it in the following screenshots:

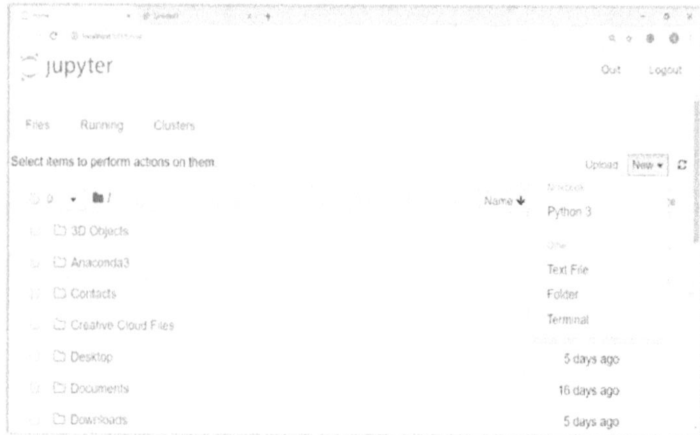

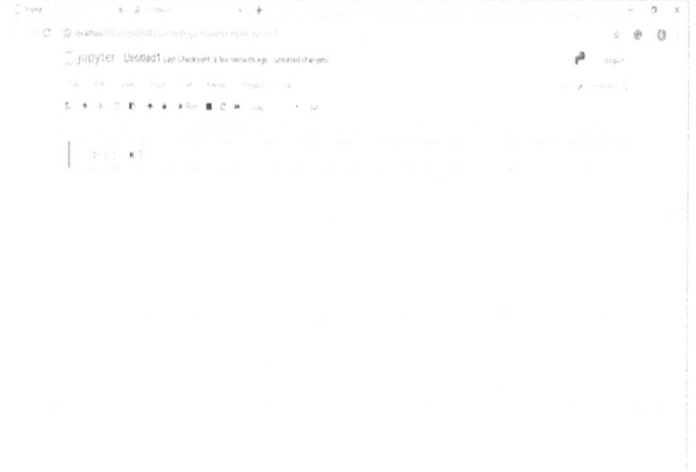

On the other hand, if you are using standard Python distribution then jupyter notebook can be installed using popular python package installer, pip.

```
pip install jupyter
```

Types of Cells in Jupyter Notebook

The following are the three types of cells in a jupyter notebook:

Code cells: As the name suggests, we can use these cells to write code. After writing the code/content, it will send it to the kernel that is associated with the notebook.

Markdown cells: We can use these cells for notating the computation process. They can contain the stuff like text, images, Latex equations, HTML tags etc.

Raw cells: The text written in them is displayed as it is. These cells are basically used to add the text that we do not wish to be converted by the automatic conversion mechanism of jupyter notebook.

NumPy

It is another useful component that makes Python as one of the favorite languages for Data Science. It basically stands for Numerical Python and consists of multidimensional array objects. By using NumPy, we can perform the following important operations:

- Mathematical and logical operations on arrays.
- Fourier transformation
- Operations associated with linear algebra.

We can also see NumPy as the replacement of MatLab because NumPy is mostly used along with Scipy (Scientific Python) and Mat-plotlib (plotting library).

Installation and Execution

If you are using Anaconda distribution, then no need to install NumPy separately as it is already installed with it. You just need to import the package into your Python script with the help of following:

```
import numpy as np
```

On the other hand, if you are using standard Python distribution then NumPy can be installed using popular python package installer, pip.

```
pip install NumPy
```

After installing NumPy, you can import it into your Python script as you did above.

Pandas

It is another useful Python library that makes Python one of the favorite languages for Data Science. Pandas is basically used for data manipulation, wrangling and analysis. It was developed by Wes McKinney in 2008. With the help of Pandas, in data processing we can accomplish the following five steps:

- Load
- Prepare
- Manipulate
- Model
- Analyze

Data representation in Pandas

The entire representation of data in Pandas is done with the help of following three data structures:

Series: It is basically a one-dimensional array with an axis label which means it is like a simple array with homogeneous data. For example, the following series is a collection of integers 1,5,10,15,24,25...

1	5	10	15	24	25	28	36	40	89

Data frame: It is the most useful data structure and used for almost all kind of data representation and manipulation in pandas. It is basically a two-dimensional data structure which can contain heterogeneous data. Generally, tabular data is represented by using data frames. For example, the following table shows the data of students having their names and roll numbers, age and gender:

Name	Roll number	Age	Gender
Aarav	1	15	Male
Harshit	2	14	Male
Kanika	3	16	Female
Mayank	4	15	Male

Panel: It is a 3-dimensional data structure containing heterogeneous data. It is very difficult to represent the panel in graphical representation, but it can be illustrated as a container of DataFrame.

The following table gives us the dimension and description about above mentioned data structures used in Pandas:

Data Structure	Dimension	Description
Series	1-D	Size immutable, 1-D homogeneous data
DataFrames	2-D	Size Mutable, Heterogeneous data in tabular form
Panel	3-D	Size-mutable array, container of DataFrame.

We can understand these data structures as the higher dimensional data structure is the container of lower dimensional data structure.

Installation and Execution

If you are using Anaconda distribution, then no need to install Pandas separately as it is already installed with it. You just need to import the package into your Python script with the help of following:

```
import pandas as pd
```

On the other hand, if you are using standard Python distribution then Pandas can be installed using popular python package installer, pip.

```
pip install Pandas
```

After installing Pandas, you can import it into your Python script as did above.

Example

The following is an example of creating a series from ndarray by using Pandas:

```
In [1]: import pandas as pd
In [2]: import numpy as np
In [3]: data = np.array(['g','a','u','r','a','v'])
In [4]: s = pd.Series(data)
In [5]: print (s)
0    g
1    a
2    u
3    r
```

```
4    a
5    v
dtype: object
```

Scikit-learn

Another useful and most important python library for Data-Science and machine learning in Python is Scikit-learn. The following are some features of Scikit-learn that makes it so useful:

- It is built on NumPy, SciPy, and Matplotlib.
- It is an open source and can be reused under BSD license.
- It is accessible to everybody and can be reused in various contexts.
- Wide range of machine learning algorithms covering major areas of ML like classification, clustering, regression, dimensionality reduction, model selection etc. can be implemented with the help of it.

Installation and Execution

If you are using Anaconda distribution, then no need to install Scikit-learn separately as it is already installed with it. You just need to use the package into your Python script. For example, with following line of script we are importing dataset of breast cancer patients from **Scikit-learn**:

```
from sklearn.datasets import load_breast_cancer
```

On the other hand, if you are using standard Python distri-bution and having NumPy and SciPy then Scikit-learn can be installed using popular python package installer, pip.

```
pip install -U scikit-learn
```

After installing Scikit-learn, you can use it into your Python script as you have done above.

Methods for Machine Learning

There are various ML algorithms, techniques and methods that can be used to build models for solving real-life problems by using data. In this chapter, we are going to discuss such different kinds of methods.

Different Types of Methods

The following are various ML methods based on some broad categories:

Based on human supervision

In the learning process, some of the methods that are based on human supervision are as follows:

Supervised Learning

Supervised learning algorithms or methods are the most commonly used ML algorithms. This method or learning algorithm take the data sample i.e. the training data and its associated output i.e. labels or responses with each data samples during the training process.

The main objective of supervised learning algorithms is to learn an association between input data samples and corresponding outputs after performing multiple training data instances.

For example, we have **x:** Input variables and **Y:** Output variable

Now, apply an algorithm to learn the mapping function from the input to output as follows:

```
Y=f(x)
```

Now, the main objective would be to approximate the mapping function so well that even when we have new input data (x), we can easily predict the output variable (Y) for that new input data.

It is called supervised because the whole process of learning can be thought as it is being supervised by a teacher or supervisor. Examples of supervised machine learning algorithms includes **Decision tree, Random Forest, KNN, Logistic Regression** etc.

Based on the ML tasks, supervised learning algorithms can be divided into following two broad classes:

- Classification
- Regression

Classification

The key objective of classification-based tasks is to predict categorial output labels or responses for the given input data. The output will be based on what the model has learned in training phase. As we know that the categorial output responses means unordered and discrete values, hence each output response will belong to a specific class or category. We will discuss Classification and associated algorithms in detail in the upcoming chapters also.

Regression

The key objective of regression-based tasks is to predict output labels or responses which are continues numeric values, for the given input data. The output will be based on what the model has learned in its training phase. Basically, regression models use the input data features (independent variables) and their corresponding continuous numeric output values (dependent or outcome variables) to learn specific association between inputs and corresponding outputs. We will discuss regression and associated algorithms in detail in further chapters also.

Unsupervised Learning

As the name suggests, it is opposite to supervised ML methods or algorithms which means in unsupervised machine learning algorithms we do not have any supervisor to provide any sort of guidance. Unsupervised learning algorithms are handy in the scenario in which we do not have the liberty, like in supervised learning algorithms, of having prelabeled training data and we want to extract useful pattern from input data.

For example, it can be understood as follows: Suppose we have:

x: Input variables, then there would be no corresponding output variable and the algorithms need to discover the interesting pattern in data for learning.

Examples of unsupervised machine learning algorithms includes **K-means clustering, K- nearest neighbors** etc.

Based on the ML tasks, unsupervised learning algorithms can be divided into following broad classes:

- Clustering
- Association
- Dimensionality Reduction

Clustering

Clustering methods are one of the most useful unsupervised ML methods. These algorithms used to find similarity as well as relationship patterns among data samples and then cluster those samples into groups having similarity based on features. The real-world example of clustering is to group the customers by their purchasing behavior.

Association

Another useful unsupervised ML method is **Association** which is used to analyze large dataset to find patterns which further represents the interesting relationships between various items. It is also termed as **Association Rule Mining** or **Market**

basket analysis which is mainly used to analyze customer shopping patterns.

Dimensionality Reduction

This unsupervised ML method is used to reduce the number of feature variables for each data sample by selecting set of principal or representative features. A question arises here is that why we need to reduce the dimensionality? The reason behind is the problem of feature space complexity which arises when we start analyzing and extracting millions of features from data samples. This problem generally refers to "curse of dimensionality". PCA (Principal Component Analysis), K-nearest neighbors and discriminant analysis are some of the popular algorithms for this purpose.

Anomaly Detection

This unsupervised ML method is used to find out the occurrences of rare events or observations that generally do not occur. By using the learned knowledge, anomaly detection methods would be able to differentiate between anomalous or a normal data point. Some of the unsupervised algorithms like clustering, KNN can detect anomalies based on the data and its features.

Semi-supervised Learning

Such kind of algorithms or methods are neither fully supervised nor fully unsupervised. They basically fall between the two i.e. supervised and unsupervised learning methods.

These kinds of algorithms generally use small supervised learning component i.e. small amount of prelabeled annotated data and large unsupervised learning component i.e. lots of unlabeled data for training. We can follow any of the following approaches for implementing semi-supervised learning methods:

- The first and simple approach is to build the supervised model based on small amount of labeled and annotated data and then build the unsupervised model by applying the same to the large amounts of unlabeled data to get more labeled samples. Now, train the model on them and repeat the process.
- The second approach needs some extra efforts. In this approach, we can first use the unsupervised methods to cluster similar data samples, annotate these groups and then use a combination of this information to train the model.

Reinforcement Learning

These methods are different from previously studied methods and very rarely used also. In this kind of learning algorithms, there would be an agent that we want to train over a period of time so that it can interact with a specific environment. The agent will follow a set of strategies for interacting with the environment and then after observing the environment it will take actions regards the current state of the environment.The following are the main steps of reinforcement learning methods:

- **Step 1:** First, we need to prepare an agent with some initial set of strategies.
- **Step 2:** Then observe the environment and its current state.
- **Step 3:** Next, select the optimal policy regards the current state of the environment and perform important action.
- **Step 4:** Now, the agent can get corresponding reward or penalty as per accordance with the action taken by it in previous step.
- **Step 5:** Now, we can update the strategies if it is required so.
- **Step 6:** At last, repeat steps 2–5 until the agent got to learn and adopt the optimal policies.

Tasks Suited for Machine Learning

The following diagram shows what type of task is appropriate for various ML problems:

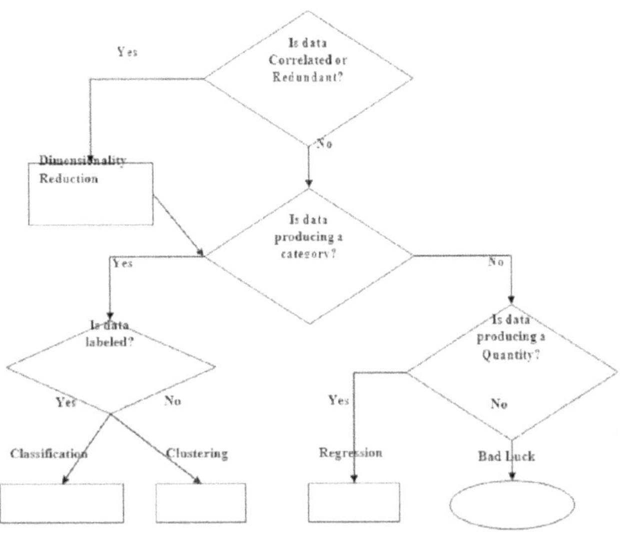

Based on learning ability

In the learning process, the following are some methods that are based on learning ability:

Batch Learning

In many cases, we have end-to-end Machine Learning systems in which we need to train the model in one go by using whole available training data. Such kind of learning method or algorithm is called **Batch or Offline learning**. It is called Batch or Offline learning because it is a one-time procedure and the model will be trained with data in one single batch. The following are the main steps of Batch learning methods:

- **Step 1:** First, we need to collect all the training data for start training the model.

- **Step 2:** Now, start the training of model by providing whole training data in one go.
- **Step 3:** Next, stop learning/training process once you got satisfactory results/performance.
- **Step 4:** Finally, deploy this trained model into production. Here, it will predict the output for new data sample.

Online Learning

It is completely opposite to the batch or offline learning methods. In these learning methods, the training data is supplied in multiple incremental batches, called mini- batches, to the algorithm. Followings are the main steps of Online learning methods:

- **Step 1:** First, we need to collect all the training data for starting training of the model.
- **Step 2:** Now, start the training of model by providing a mini-batch of training data to the algorithm.
- **Step 3:** Next, we need to provide the mini-batches of training data in multiple increments to the algorithm.
- **Step 4:** As it will not stop like batch learning hence after providing whole training data in mini-batches, provide new data samples also to it.
- **Step 5:** Finally, it will keep learning over a period of time based on the new data samples.

Based on Generalization Approach

In the learning process, followings are some methods that are based on generalization approaches:

Instance based Learning

Instance based learning method is one of the useful methods that build the ML models by doing generalization based on the input data. It is opposite to the previously studied learning methods in the way that this kind of learning involves ML systems as well as methods that uses the raw data points themselves to draw the outcomes for newer data samples without building an explicit model on training data.

In simple words, instance-based learning basically starts working by looking at the input data points and then using a similarity metric, it will generalize and predict the new data points.

Model based Learning

In Model based learning methods, an iterative process takes place on the ML models that are built based on various model parameters, called hyper parameters and in which input data is used to extract the features. In this learning, hyper parameters are optimized based on various model validation techniques. That is why we can say that Model based learning methods uses more traditional ML approach towards generalization.

Data Loading for ML Projects

Suppose if you want to start a ML project then what is the first and most important thing you would require? It is the data that we need to load for starting any of the ML project. With respect to data, the most common format of data for ML projects is CSV (comma- separated values).

Basically, CSV is a simple file format which is used to store tabular data (number and text) such as a spreadsheet in plain text. In Python, we can load CSV data into with different ways but before loading CSV data we must have to take care about some considerations.

Consideration While Loading CSV data

CSV data format is the most common format for ML data, but we need to take care about following major considerations while loading the same into our ML projects:

File Header

In CSV data files, the header contains the information for each field. We must use the same delimiter for the header file and for data file because it is the header file that specifies how should data fields be interpreted.

The following are the two cases related to CSV file header which must be considered:

- **Case-I: When Data file is having a file header:** It will automatically assign the names to each column of data if data file is having a file header.
- **Case-II: When Data file is not having a file header:** We need to assign the names to each column of data manually if data file is not having a file header.

In both the cases, we must need to specify explicitly weather our CSV file contains header or not.

Comments

Comments in any data file are having their significance. In CSV data file, comments are indicated by a hash (#) at the start of the line. We need to consider comments while loading CSV data into ML projects because if we are having comments in the file then we may need to indicate, depends upon the method we choose for loading, whether to expect those comments or not.

Delimiter

In CSV data files, comma (,) character is the standard delimiter. The role of delimiter is to separate the values in the fields. It is important to consider the role of delimiter while uploading the

CSV file into ML projects because we can also use a different delimiter such as a tab or white space. But in the case of using a different delimiter than standard one, we must have to specify it explicitly.

Quotes

In CSV data files, double quotation ("") mark is the default quote character. It is important to consider the role of quotes while uploading the CSV file into ML projects because we can also use other quote character than double quotation mark. But in case of using a different quote character than standard one, we must have to specify it explicitly.

Methods to Load CSV Data File

While working with ML projects, the most crucial task is to load the data properly into it. The most common data format for ML projects is CSV and it comes in various flavors and varying difficulties to parse. In this section, we are going to discuss about three common approaches in Python to load CSV data file:

Load CSV with Python Standard Library

The first and most used approach to load CSV data file is the use of Python standard library which provides us a variety of built-in modules namely **csv module** and the **reader()function**. The following is an example of loading CSV data file with the help of it:

Example

In this example, we are using the iris flower data set which can be downloaded into our local directory. After loading the data file, we can convert it into **NumPy** array and use it for ML projects. Following is the Python script for loading CSV data file:

First, we need to import the csv module provided by Python standard library as follows:

```
import csv
```

Next, we need to import Numpy module for converting the loaded data into NumPy array.

```
import numpy as np
```

Now, provide the full path of the file, stored on our local directory, having the CSV data file:

```
path = r"c:\iris.csv"
```

Next, use the csv.reader()function to read data from CSV file:

```
with open(path,'r') as f:
reader = csv.reader(f,delimiter = ',')
headers = next(reader)
data = list(reader)
data = np.array(data).astype(float)
```

We can print the names of the headers with the following line of script:

```
print(headers)
```

The following line of script will print the shape of the data i.e. number of rows & columns in the file:

```
print(data.shape)
```

Next script line will give the first three line of data file:

```
print(data[:3])
```

Output

['sepal_length', 'sepal_width', 'petal_length', 'petal_width']
  (150, 4)
   [[5.1 3.5 1.4 0.2]
   [4.9 3. 1.4 0.2]
   [4.7 3.2 1.3 0.2]]

Load CSV with NumPy

Another approach to load CSV data file is **NumPy**and **numpy.loadtxt() function**. The following is an example of loading CSV data file with the help of it:

Example

In this example, we are using the Pima Indians Dataset having the data of diabetic patients. This dataset is a numeric dataset with no header. It can also be downloaded into our local directory. After loading the data file, we can convert it into **NumPy** array and use it for ML projects. The following is the Python script for loading CSV data file:

```
from numpy import loadtxt
path = r"C:\pima-indians-diabetes.csv" datapath=
open(path, 'r')
data = loadtxt(datapath, delimiter=",")
print(data.shape)
print(data[:3])
```

Output

```
(768, 9)

[[ 6.     148.     72.     35.      0.     33.6     0.627   50.      1.]
 [ 1.      85.     66.     29.      0.     26.6     0.351   31.      0.]
 [ 8.     183.     64.      0.      0.     23.3     0.672   32.      1.]]
```

Load CSV with Pandas

Another approach to load CSV data file is by **Pandas** and **pandas.read_csv()function**. This is the very flexible function that returns a **pandas.DataFrame** which can be used immediately for plotting. The following is an example of loading CSV data file with the help of it:

Example

Here, we will be implementing two Python scripts, first is with Iris data set having headers and another is by using the Pima Indians Dataset which is a numeric dataset with no header. Both the datasets can be downloaded into local directory.

Script-1

The following is the Python script for loading CSV data file using **Pandas** on Iris Data set:

```
from pandas import read_csv
path = r"C:\iris.csv"
data = read_csv(path)
print(data.shape)
print(data[:3])


Output:


(150, 4)
   sepal_length        sepal_width   petal_length    petal_width
0          5.1          3.5           1.4            0.2
1          4.9          3.0           1.4            0.2
2          4.7          3.2           1.3            0.2
```

Script-2

The following is the Python script for loading CSV data file, along with providing the headers names too, using Pandas on Pima Indians Diabetes dataset:

```
from pandas import read_csv
path = r"C:\pima-indians-diabetes.csv"
headernames = ['preg', 'plas', 'pres', 'skin',
'test', 'mass', 'pedi', 'age',
```

```
'class']
data = read_csv(path, names=headernames)
print(data.shape)
print(data[:3])
```

Output

```
(768, 9)
   preg  plas  pres  skin  test  mass   pedi  age  class
0     6   148    72    35     0  33.6  0.627   50      1
1     1    85    66    29     0  26.6  0.351   31      0
2     8   183    64     0     0  23.3  0.672   32      1
```

The difference between above used three approaches for loading CSV data file can easily be understood with the help of given examples.

Understanding Data with Statistics

While working with machine learning projects, usually we ignore two most important parts called **mathematics** and **data**. It is because, we know that ML is a data driven approach and our ML model will produce only as good or as bad results as the data we provided to it.

In the previous chapter, we discussed how we can upload CSV data into our ML project, but it would be good to understand the data before uploading it. We can understand the data by two ways, with statistics and with visualization.

In this chapter, with the help of following Python recipes, we are going to understand ML data with statistics.

Looking at Raw Data

The very first recipe is for looking at your raw data. It is important to look at raw data because the insight we will get after looking at raw data will boost our chances to better pre-processing as well as handling of data for ML projects.

Following is a Python script implemented by using head() function of Pandas DataFrame on Pima Indians diabetes dataset to look at the first 50 rows to get better understanding of it:

Example

```python
from pandas import read_csv
path = r"C:\pima-indians-diabetes.csv"
headernames = ['preg', 'plas', 'pres', 'skin',
'test', 'mass', 'pedi', 'age',
'class']
data = read_csv(path, names=headernames)
print(data.head(50))
```

Output

```
    preg    plas    pres  skin  test  mass  pedi    age
class
0          6     148    72    35     0    33.6  0.627
50                1
1          1      85    66    29     0    26.6  0.351
31                0
2          8     183    64     0     0    23.3  0.672
32                1
3          1      89    66    23    94    28.1  0.167
21                0
4          0     137    40    35   168    43.1  2.288
33                1
5          5     116    74     0     0    25.6  0.201
30                0
6          3      78    50    32    88    31.0  0.248
26                1
7         10     115     0     0     0    35.3  0.134
```

29							
		0					
8	2	197	70	45	543	30.5	0.158
53		1					
9	8	125	96	0	0	0.0	0.232
54		1					
10	4	110	92	0	0	37.6	0.191
30		0					
11	10	168	74	0	0	38.0	0.537
34		1					
12	10	139	80	0	0	27.1	1.441
57		0					
13	1	189	60	23	846	30.1	0.398
59		1					
14	5	166	72	19	175	25.8	0.587
51		1					
15	7	100	0	0	0	30.0	0.484
32		1					
16	0	118	84	47	230	45.8	0.551
31		1					
17	7	107	74	0	0	29.6	0.254
31		1					
18	1	103	30	38	83	43.3	0.183
33		0					
19	1	115	70	30	96	34.6	0.529
32		1					
20	3	126	88	41	235	39.3	0.704
27		0					
21	8	99	84	0	0	35.4	0.388
50		0					
22	7	196	90	0	0	39.8	0.451
41		1					
23	9	119	80	35	0	29.0	0.263
29		1					
24	11	143	94	33	146	36.6	0.254
51		1					
25	10	125	70	26	115	31.1	0.205
41		1					

26	7	147	76	0	0	39.4	0.257	43	1
27	1	97	66	15	140	23.2	0.487	22	0
28	13	145	82	19	110	22.2	0.245	57	0
29	5	117	92	0	0	34.1	0.337	38	0
30	5	109	75	26	0	36.0	0.546	60	0
31	3	158	76	36	245	31.6	0.851	28	1
32	3	88	58	11	54	24.8	0.267	22	0
33	6	92	92	0	0	19.9	0.188	28	0
34	10	122	78	31	0	27.6	0.512	45	0
35	4	103	60	33	192	24.0	0.966	33	0
36	11	138	76	0	0	33.2	0.420	35	0
37	9	102	76	37	0	32.9	0.665	46	1
38	2	90	68	42	0	38.2	0.503	27	1
39	4	111	72	47	207	37.1	1.390	56	1
40	3	180	64	25	70	34.0	0.271	26	0
41	7	133	84	0	0	40.2	0.696	37	0
42	7	106	92	18	0	22.7	0.235	48	0
43	9	171	110	24	240	45.4	0.721	54	1
44	7	159	64	0	0	27.4	0.294		

```
40            0
45     0     180    66    39    0    42.0  1.893
25            1
46     1     146    56     0    0    29.7  0.564
29            0
47     2      71    70    27    0    28.0  0.586
22            0
48     7     103    66    32    0    39.1  0.344
31            1
49     7     105     0     0    0     0.0  0.305
24            0
```

We can observe from the above output that first column gives the row number which can be very useful for referencing a specific observation.

Checking Dimensions of Data

It is always a good practice to know how much data, in terms of rows and columns, we are having for our ML project. The reasons behind are:

- Suppose if we have too many rows and columns then it would take long time to run the algorithm and train the model.
- Suppose if we have too less rows and columns then it we would not have enough data to well train the model.

Following is a Python script implemented by printing the **shape** property on Pandas Data Frame. We are going to implement it on iris data set for getting the total number of rows and columns in it.

Example

```
from pandas import read_csv path= r"C:\iris.csv"
data = read_csv(path)
print(data.shape)
```

Output

```
(150, 4)
```

We can easily observe from the output that iris data set, we are going to use, is having 150 rows and 4 columns.

Getting Each Attribute's Data Type

It is another good practice to know data type of each attribute. The reason behind is that, as per to the requirement, sometimes we may need to convert one data type to another. For example, we may need to convert string into floating point or int for representing categorial or ordinal values. We can have an idea about the attribute's data type by looking at the raw data, but another way is to use **dtypes** property of Pandas DataFrame. With the help of **dtypes**property we can categorize each attributes data type. It can be understood with the help of following Python script:

Example

```
from pandas import read_csv path= r"C:\iris.csv"
data = read_csv(path)
```

```
print(data.dtypes)
```

Output

```
sepal_length float64
sepal_width float64
petal_length float64
petal_width   float64
dtype: object
```

From the above output, we can easily get the datatypes of each attribute.

Statistical Summary of Data

We have discussed Python recipe to get the shape i.e. number of rows and columns, of data but many times we need to review the summaries out of that shape of data. It can be done with the help of **describe()** function of Pandas DataFrame that further provide the following 8 statistical properties of each & every data attribute:

- Count
- Mean
- Standard Deviation
- Minimum Value
- Maximum value
- 25%
- Median i.e. 50%
- 75%

Example

```python
from pandas import read_csv from pandas import
set_option
path = r"C:\pima-indians-diabetes.csv"
names = ['preg', 'plas', 'pres', 'skin', 'test',
'mass', 'pedi', 'age',
'class']
data = read_csv(path, names=names)
set_option('display.width', 100)
set_option('precision', 2) print(data.shape)
print(data.describe())
```

Output

```
(768, 9)
           preg     plas    pres    skin     test    mass    pedi     age   class
count    768.00   768.00  768.00  768.00   768.00  768.00  768.00  768.00  768.00
mean       3.85   120.89   69.11   20.54    79.80   31.99    0.47   33.24    0.35
std        3.37    31.97   19.36   15.95   115.24    7.88    0.33   11.76    0.48
min        0.00     0.00    0.00    0.00     0.00    0.00    0.08   21.00    0.00
25%        1.00    99.00   62.00    0.00     0.00   27.30    0.24   24.00    0.00
50%        3.00   117.00   72.00   23.00    30.50   32.00    0.37   29.00    0.00
75%        6.00   140.25   80.00   32.00   127.25   36.60    0.63   41.00    1.00
max       17.00   199.00  122.00   99.00   846.00   67.10    2.42   81.00    1.00
```

From the above output, we can observe the statistical summary of the data of Pima Indian Diabetes dataset along with shape of data.

Reviewing Class Distribution

Class distribution statistics is useful in classification problems where we need to know the balance of class values. It is important to know class value distribution because if we have highly imbalanced class distribution i.e. one class is having lots more observations than other class, then it may need special handling at data preparation stage of our ML project. We can easily get class distribution in Python with the help of Pandas DataFrame.

Example

```
from pandas import read_csv
path = r"C:\pima-indians-diabetes.csv"
names = ['preg', 'plas', 'pres', 'skin', 'test',
'mass', 'pedi', 'age',
'class']
data = read_csv(path, names=names)
count_class = data.groupby('class').size()
print(count_class)
```

Output:

```
Class
0    500
1    268
dtype: int64
```

From the above output, it can be clearly seen that the number of observations with class 0 are almost double than number of observations with class 1.

Reviewing Correlation between Attributes

The relationship between two variables is called correlation.

In statistics, the most common method for calculating correlation is Pearson's Correlation Coefficient. It can have three values as follows:

- **Coefficient value = 1:** It represents full **positive** correlation between variables.
- **Coefficient value = -1:** It represents full **negative** correlation between variables.
- **Coefficient value = 0:** It represents **no** correlation at all between variables.

It is always good for us to review the pairwise correlations of the attributes in our dataset before using it into ML project because some machine learning algorithms such as linear regression and logistic regression will perform poorly if we have highly correlated attributes. In Python, we can easily calculate a correlation matrix of dataset attributes with the help of **corr()** function on Pandas DataFrame.

Example

```
from pandas import read_csv frompandas import
set_option
path = r"C:\pima-indians-diabetes.csv"
names = ['preg', 'plas', 'pres', 'skin', 'test',
'mass', 'pedi', 'age',
'class']
data = read_csv(path, names=names)
set_option('display.width', 100)
set_option('precision', 2)
correlations = data.corr(method='pearson')
print(correlations)
```

Output

```
preg     plas    pres    skin    test   mass  pedi    age
    class
preg     1.00     0.13     0.14   -0.08 -0.07   0.02
-0.03      0.54   0.22 plas      0.13    1.00    0.15
0.06   0.33   0.22      0.14      0.26   0.47 pres      0.14
   0.15    1.00      0.21   0.09   0.28     0.04      0.24
0.07 skin    -0.08      0.06      0.21    1.00   0.44   0.39
   0.18    -0.11    0.07 test    -0.07     0.33     0.09
0.44   1.00   0.20      0.19     -0.04    0.13 mass      0.02
   0.22     0.28     0.39   0.20   1.00      0.14      0.04
0.29
pedi     -0.03     0.14     0.04     0.18   0.19   0.14
1.00      0.03   0.17
age      0.54      0.26     0.24   -0.11 -0.04   0.04
0.03     1.00   0.24
class    0.22      0.47     0.07     0.07   0.13   0.29
0.17      0.24   1.00
```

The matrix in above output gives the correlation between all the pairs of the attribute in dataset.

Reviewing Skew of Attribute Distribution

Skewness may be defined as the distribution that is assumed to be Gaussian but appears distorted or shifted in one direction or another, or either to the left or right. Reviewing the skewness of attributes is one of the important tasks due to following reasons:

- Presence of skewness in data requires the correction at data preparation stage so that we can get more accuracy

from our model.
- Most of the ML algorithms assumes that data has a Gaussian distribution i.e. either normal of bell curved data.

In Python, we can easily calculate the skew of each attribute by using **skew()** function on Pandas DataFrame.

Example

```
from pandas import read_csv
path = r"C:\pima-indians-diabetes.csv"
names = ['preg', 'plas', 'pres', 'skin', 'test',
'mass', 'pedi', 'age',
'class']
data = read_csv(path, names=names)
print(data.skew())
```

Output

```
preg    0.90
plas    0.17
pres   -1.84
skin    0.11
test    2.27
mass   -0.43
pedi    1.92
age     1.13
class   0.64
dtype: float64
```

From the above output, positive or negative skew can be observed. If the value is closer to zero, then it shows less skew.

Understanding Data with Visualization

In the previous chapter, we have discussed the importance of data for Machine Learning algorithms along with some Python recipes to understand the data with statistics. There is another way called Visualization, to understand the data.

With the help of data visualization, we can see how the data looks like and what kind of correlation is held by the attributes of data. It is the fastest way to see if the features correspond to the output. With the help of following Python recipes, we can understand ML data with statistics.

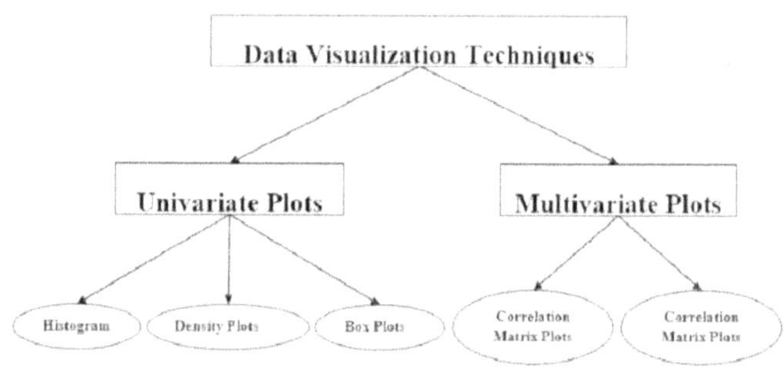

Univariate Plots: Understanding Attributes Independently

The simplest type of visualization is single-variable or "univariate" visualization. With the help of univariate visualization, we can understand each attribute of our dataset independently. The following are some techniques in Python to implement univariate visualization:

Histograms

Histograms group the data in bins and is the fastest way to get idea about the distribution of each attribute in dataset. The following are some of the characteristics of histograms:

- It provides us a count of the number of observations in each bin created for visualization.
- From the shape of the bin, we can easily observe the distribution i.e. weather it is Gaussian, skewed or exponential.
- Histograms also help us to see possible outliers.

Example

The code shown below is an example of Python script creating the histogram of the attributes of Pima Indian Diabetes dataset. Here, we will be using **hist()** function on **Pandas** DataFrame to generate histograms and **matplotlib** for ploting them.

```
from matplotlib import pyplot frompandas import
read_csv
path = r"C:\pima-indians-diabetes.csv"
names = ['preg', 'plas', 'pres', 'skin', 'test',
```

```
'mass', 'pedi', 'age',
'class']
data = read_csv(path, names=names)
data.hist()
pyplot.show()
```

Output

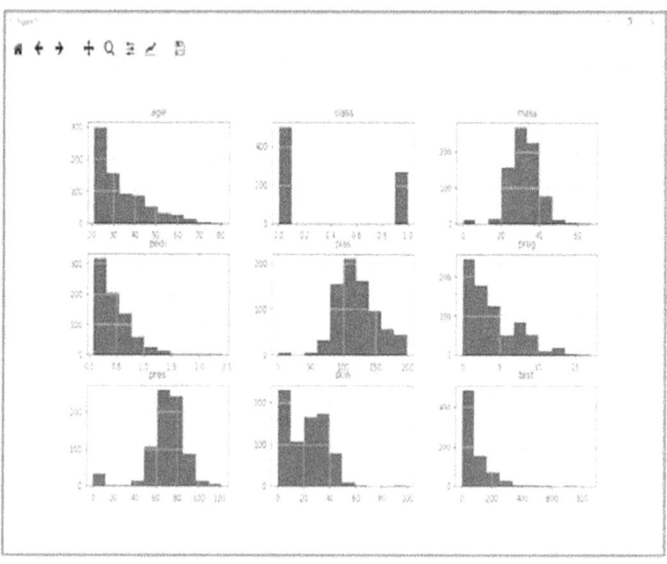

The above output shows that it created the histogram for each attribute in the dataset. From this, we can observe that perhaps age, pedi and test attribute may have exponential distribution while mass and plas have Gaussian distribution.

Density Plots

Another quick and easy technique for getting each attributes distribution is Density plots. It is also like histogram but having a smooth curve drawn through the top of each bin. We can call them as abstracted histograms.

Example

In the following example, Python script will generate Density Plots for the distribution of attributes of Pima Indian Diabetes dataset.

```python
from matplotlib import pyplot from pandas import
read_csv
path = r"C:\pima-indians-diabetes.csv"
names = ['preg', 'plas', 'pres', 'skin', 'test',
'mass', 'pedi', 'age',
'class']
data = read_csv(path, names=names)
data.plot(kind='density', subplots=True,
layout=(3,3), sharex=False)
pyplot.show()
```

Output

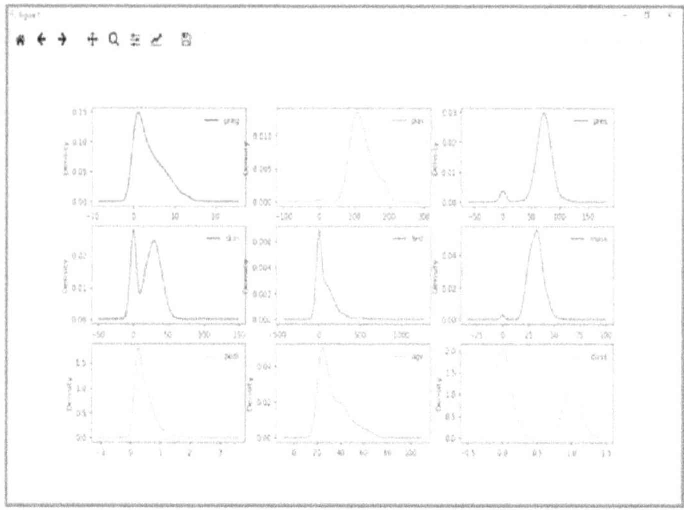

From the above output, the difference between Density plots and Histograms can be easily understood.

Box and Whisker Plots

Box and Whisker plots, also called box plots in short, is another useful technique to review the distribution of each attribute's distribution. The following are the characteristics of this technique:

- It is univariate in nature and summarizes the distribution of each attribute.
- It draws a line for the middle value i.e. for median.
- It draws a box around the 25% and 75%.
- It also draws whiskers which will give us an idea about the spread of the data.
- The dots outside the whiskers signifies the outlier values.

Outlier values would be 1.5 times greater than the size of the spread of the middle data.

Example

In the following example, Python script will generate Density Plots for the distribution of attributes of Pima Indian Diabetes dataset.

```
from matplotlib import pyplot from pandas import
read_csv
path = r"C:\pima-indians-diabetes.csv"
names = ['preg', 'plas', 'pres', 'skin', 'test',
'mass', 'pedi', 'age',
'class']
data = read_csv(path, names=names)
data.plot(kind='box', subplots=True, layout=(3,3),
sharex=False,sharey=False)
pyplot.show()
```

Output

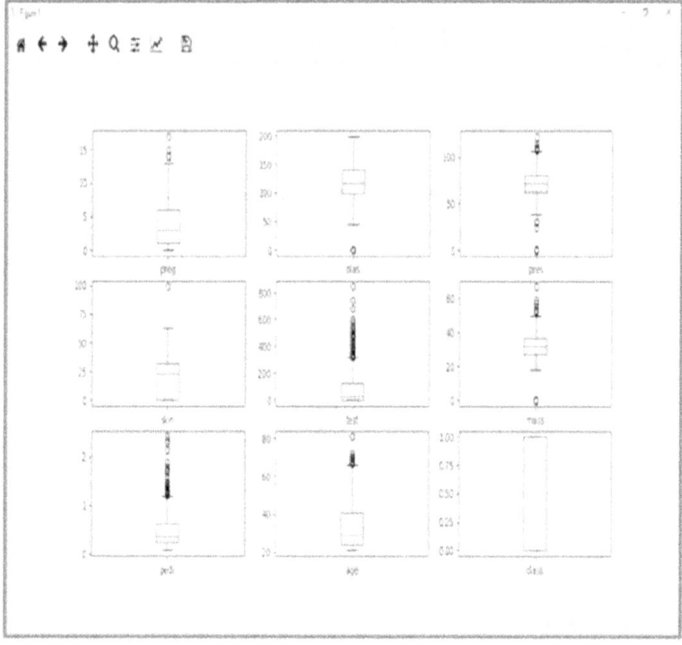

From the above plot of attribute's distribution, it can be observed that age, test and skin appear skewed towards smaller values.

Multivariate Plots: Interaction Among Multiple Variables

Another type of visualization is multi-variable or "multivariate" visualization. With the help of multivariate visualization, we can understand interaction between multiple attributes of our dataset. The following are some techniques in Python to implement multivariate visualization:

Correlation Matrix Plot

Correlation is an indication about the changes between two variables. In our previous chapters, we have discussed Pearson's Correlation coefficients and the importance of Correlation too. We can plot correlation matrix to show which variable is having a high or low correlation in respect to another variable.

Example

In the following example, Python script will generate and plot correlation matrix for the PimaIndian Diabetes dataset. It can be generated with the help of corr() function on Pandas DataFrame and plotted with the help of pyplot.

```python
from matplotlib import pyplot from pandas import
read_csv import numpy
Path = r"C:\pima-indians-diabetes.csv"
names = ['preg', 'plas', 'pres', 'skin', 'test',
'mass', 'pedi', 'age',
'class']
data = read_csv(Path, names=names)
correlations = data.corr()
fig = pyplot.figure()
ax = fig.add_subplot(111)
cax = ax.matshow(correlations,vmin=-1, vmax=1)
fig.colorbar(cax)
ticks = numpy.arange(0,9,1) ax.set_xticks(ticks)
ax.set_yticks(ticks) ax.set_xticklabels(names)
ax.set_yticklabels(names)
pyplot.show()
```

Output

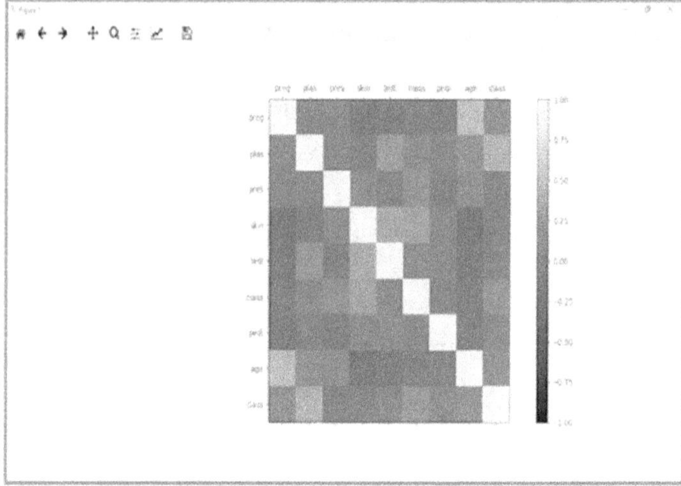

From the above output of correlation matrix, we can see that it is symmetrical i.e. the bottom left is same as the top right. It is also observed that each variable is positively correlated with each other.

Scatter Matrix Plot

Scatter plots shows how much one variable is affected by another or the relationship between them with the help of dots in two dimensions. Scatter plots are very much like line graphs in the concept that they use horizontal and vertical axes to plot data points.

Example

In the following example, Python script will generate and plot

Scatter matrix for the Pima Indian Diabetes dataset. It can be generated with the help of scatter_matrix() function on Pandas DataFrame and plotted with the help of pyplot.

```
from matplotlib import pyplot from pandas import
read_csv
from pandas.tools.plotting import scatter_matrix
path = r"C:\pima-indians-diabetes.csv"
names = ['preg', 'plas', 'pres', 'skin', 'test',
'mass', 'pedi', 'age',
'class']
data = read_csv(path, names=names)
scatter_matrix(data)
pyplot.show()
```

Output

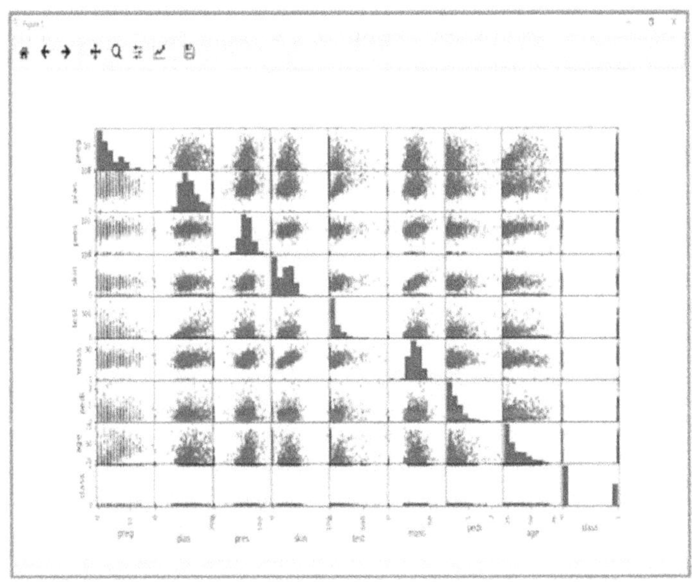

Preparing Data

Machine Learning algorithms are completely dependent on data because it is the most crucial aspect that makes model training possible. On the other hand, if we won't be able to make sense out of that data, before feeding it to ML algorithms, a machine will be useless. In simple words, we always need to feed right data i.e. the data in correct scale, format and containing meaningful features, for the problem we want machine to solve.

This makes data preparation the most important step in ML process. Data preparation may be defined as the procedure that makes our dataset more appropriate for ML process.

Why Data Pre-processing?

After selecting the raw data for ML training, the most important task is data pre- processing. In broad sense, data preprocessing will convert the selected data into a form we can work with or can feed to ML algorithms. We always need to preprocess our data so that it can be as per the expectation of machine learning algorithm.

Data Pre-processing Techniques

We have the following data preprocessing techniques that can be applied on data set to produce data for ML algorithms:

Scaling:

Most probably our dataset comprises of the attributes with varying scale, but we cannot provide such data to ML algorithm hence it requires rescaling. Data rescaling makes sure that attributes are at same scale. Generally, attributes are rescaled into the range of 0 and 1. ML algorithms like gradient descent and k-Nearest Neighbors requires scaled data. We can rescale the data with the help of **MinMaxScaler** class of **scikit-learn** Python library.

Example

In this example we will rescale the data of Pima Indians Diabetes dataset which we used earlier. First, the CSV data will be loaded (as done in the previous chapters) and then with the help of **MinMaxScaler** class, it will be rescaled in the range of 0 and 1.

The first few lines of the following script are same as we have written in previous chapters while loading CSV data.

```
from pandas import read_csv
from numpy import set_printoptions fromsklearn
import preprocessing
path = r'C:\pima-indians-diabetes.csv'
```

```
names = ['preg', 'plas', 'pres', 'skin', 'test',
'mass', 'pedi', 'age',
'class']
dataframe = read_csv(path, names=names)
array = dataframe.values
```

Now, we can use **MinMaxScaler** class to rescale the data in the range of 0 and 1.

```
data_scaler =
preprocessing.MinMaxScaler(feature_range=(0,1))
data_rescaled = data_scaler.fit_transform(array)
```

We can also summarize the data for output as per our choice. Here, we are setting the precision to 1 and showing the first 10 rows in the output.

```
set_printoptions(precision=1)
print ("\nScaled data:\n", data_rescaled[0:10])
```

Output

```
Scaled data:
[[0.4 0.7 0.6  0.4  0.   0.5   0.2  0.5  1.]
 [0.1 0.4  0.5  0.3  0.   0.4  0.1  0.2  0. ]
 [0.5 0.9  0.5  0.   0.   0.3  0.3  0.2  1. ]
 [0.1 0.4  0.5  0.2  0.1  0.4  0.   0.   0. ]
 [0.   0.7  0.3  0.4  0.2  0.6  0.9  0.2  1. ]
 [0.3 0.6  0.6  0.   0.   0.4  0.1  0.2  0. ]
 [0.2 0.4  0.4  0.3  0.1  0.5  0.1  0.1  1. ]
 [0.6 0.6  0.   0.   0.   0.5  0.   0.1  0. ]
 [0.1 1.   0.6  0.5  0.6  0.5  0.   0.5  1. ]
```

```
 [0.5 0.6 0.8 0.   0.   0.   0.1 0.6  1.]]
```

From the above output, all the data got rescaled into the range of 0 and 1.

Normalization

Another useful data preprocessing technique is Normalization. This is used to rescale each row of data to have a length of 1. It is mainly useful in Sparse dataset where we have lots of zeros. We can rescale the data with the help of **Normalizer** class of **scikit-learn** Python library.

Types of Normalization

In machine learning, there are two types of normalization preprocessing techniques as follows:

L1 Normalization

It may be defined as the normalization technique that modifies the dataset values in a way that in each row the sum of the absolute values will always be up to 1. It is also called Least Absolute Deviations.

Example

In this example, we use L1 Normalize technique to normalize the data of Pima Indians Diabetes dataset which we used earlier. First, the CSV data will be loaded and then with the help of **Normalizer** class it will be normalized.

The first few lines of following script are same as we have written in previous chapters while loading CSV data.

```
from pandas import read_csv
from numpy import set_printoptions
from sklearn.preprocessing import Normalizer path =
r'C:\pima-indians-diabetes.csv'
names = ['preg', 'plas', 'pres', 'skin', 'test',
'mass', 'pedi', 'age',
'class']
dataframe = read_csv (path, names=names)
array = dataframe.values
```

Now, we can use Normalizer class with L1 to normalize the data.

```
Data_normalizer = Normalizer(norm='l1').fit(array)
Data_normalized = Data_normalizer.transform(array)
```

We can also summarize the data for output as per our choice. Here, we are setting the precision to 2 and showing the first 3 rows in the output.

```
set_printoptions(precision=2)
print ("\nNormalized data:\n", Data_normalized [0:3])
```

Output

```
Normalized data:
```

```
[[0.02    0.43    0.21    0.1  0.  0.1    0.    0.14    0.]
 [0.      0.36    0.28    0.12 0.  0.11   0.    0.13    0.]
 [0.03    0.59    0.21    0.   0.  0.07   0.    0.10.   0]]
```

L2 Normalization

It may be defined as the normalization technique that modifies the dataset values in a way that in each row the sum of the squares will always be up to 1. It is also called least squares.

Example

In this example, we use L2 Normalization technique to normalize the data of Pima Indians Diabetes dataset which we used earlier. First, the CSV data will be loaded (as done in previous chapters) and then with the help of **Normalizer** class it will be normalized.

The first few lines of following script are same as we have written in previous chapters while loading CSV data.

```
from pandas import read_csv
from numpy import set_printoptions
from sklearn.preprocessing import Normalizer path =
r'C:\pima-indians-diabetes.csv'
names = ['preg', 'plas', 'pres', 'skin', 'test',
'mass', 'pedi', 'age',
'class']
dataframe = read_csv (path, names=names)
array = dataframe.values
```

Now, we can use **Normalizer** class with L1 to normalize the data.

```
Data_normalizer = Normalizer(norm='l2').fit(array)
Data_normalized = Data_normalizer.transform(array)
```

We can also summarize the data for output as per our choice. Here, we are setting the precision to 2 and showing the first 3 rows in the output.

```
set_printoptions(precision=2)
print ("\nNormalized data:\n", Data_normalized [0:3])
```

Output

```
Normalized data:
[[0.03  0.83  0.4   0.2   0.  0.19 0. 0.28  0.01]
 [0.01  0.72  0.56  0.24  0.  0.22 0. 0.26  0. ]
 [0.04  0.92  0.32  0.    0.  0.12 0. 0.16  0.01]]
```

Binarization

As the name suggests, this is the technique with the help of which we can make our data binary. We can use a binary threshold for making our data binary. The values above that threshold value will be converted to 1 and below that threshold will be converted to 0.

For example, if we choose threshold value = 0.5, then the dataset value above it will become 1 and below this will become 0. That is why we can call it **binarizing** the data or **thresholding** the data. This technique is useful when we have probabilities in our dataset and want to convert them into crisp values.

We can binarize the data with the help of **Binarizer** class of **scikit-learn** Python library.

Example

In this example, we will rescale the data of Pima Indians Diabetes dataset which we used earlier. First, the CSV data will be loaded and then with the help of **Binarizer** class it will be converted into binary values i.e. 0 and 1 depending upon the threshold value. We are taking 0.5 as threshold value.

The first few lines of following script are same as we have written in previous chapters while loading CSV data.

```
from pandas import read_csv
from sklearn.preprocessing import Binarizer path =
r'C:\pima-indians-diabetes.csv'
names = ['preg', 'plas', 'pres', 'skin', 'test',
'mass', 'pedi', 'age',
'class']
dataframe = read_csv(path, names=names)
array = dataframe.values
```

Now, we can use **Binarize** class to convert the data into binary values.

```
binarizer = Binarizer(threshold=0.5).fit(array)
Data_binarized = binarizer.transform(array)
```

Here, we are showing the first 5 rows in the output.

```python
print ("\nBinary data:\n", Data_binarized [0:5])
```

Output

```
Binary data:
[[1. 1. 1. 1. 0. 1. 1. 1. 1.]
 [1.  1. 1. 1. 0. 1. 0. 1. 0.]
 [1.  1. 1. 0. 0. 1. 1. 1. 1.]
 [1.  1. 1. 1. 1. 1. 0. 1. 0.]
 [0.  1. 1. 1. 1. 1. 1. 1. 1.]]
```

Standardization

Another useful data preprocessing technique which is basically used to transform the data attributes with a Gaussian distribution. It differs the mean and SD (Standard Deviation) to a standard Gaussian distribution with a mean of 0 and a SD of 1. This technique is useful in ML algorithms like linear regression, logistic regression that assumes a Gaussian distribution in input dataset and produce better results with rescaled data. We can standardize the data (mean = 0 and SD =1) with the help of **StandardScaler** class of **scikit-learn** Python library.

Example

In this example, we will rescale the data of Pima Indians Diabetes dataset which we used earlier. First, the CSV data will be loaded and then with the help of **StandardScaler** class it will be converted into Gaussian Distribution with mean = 0 and SD = 1.

The first few lines of following script are same as we have written in previous chapters while loading CSV data.

```
from sklearn.preprocessing import StandardScaler
from pandas import read_csv
from numpy import set_printoptions
path = r'C:\pima-indians-diabetes.csv'
names = ['preg', 'plas', 'pres', 'skin', 'test',
'mass', 'pedi', 'age',
'class']
dataframe = read_csv(path, names=names)
array = dataframe.values
```

Now, we can use **StandardScaler** class to rescale the data.

```
data_scaler = StandardScaler().fit(array)
data_rescaled = data_scaler.transform(array)
```

We can also summarize the data for output as per our choice. Here, we are setting the precision to 2 and showing the first 5 rows in the output.

```
set_printoptions(precision=2)
print ("\nRescaled data:\n", data_rescaled [0:5])
```

Output

```
Rescaled data:
[[ 0.64  0.85  0.15   0.91  -0.69  0.2   0.47  1.43
```

```
   1.37]
 [-0.84    -1.12 -0.16  0.53  -0.69 -0.68 -0.37 -0.19
 -0.73]
 [ 1.23     1.94 -0.26 -1.29  -0.69 -1.1   0.6  -0.11
  1.37]
 [-0.84    -1.   -0.16  0.15   0.12 -0.49 -0.92 -1.04
 -0.73]
 [-1.14     0.5  -1.5   0.91   0.77  1.41  5.48 -0.02
  1.37]]
```

Data Labeling

We discussed the importance of good fata for ML algorithms
as well as some techniques to pre-process the data before
sending it to ML algorithms. One more aspect in this regard
is data labeling. It is also very important to send the data to
ML algorithms having proper labeling. For example, in case
of classification problems, lot of labels in the form of words,
numbers etc. are there on the data.

What is Label Encoding?

Most of the **sklearn** functions expect that the data with number
labels rather than word labels. Hence, we need to convert
such labels into number labels. This process is called label
encoding. We can perform label encoding of data with the help
of **LabelEncoder()** function of **scikit-learn** Python library.

Example

In the following example, Python script will perform the

label encoding. First, import the required Python libraries as follows:

```
import numpy as np
from sklearn import preprocessing
Now, we need to provide the input labels as follows:
input_labels =
['red','black','red','green','black','yellow','white']
```

The next line of code will create the label encoder and train it.

```
encoder = preprocessing.LabelEncoder()
encoder.fit(input_labels)
```

The next lines of script will check the performance by encoding the random ordered list:

```
test_labels = ['green','red','black'] encoded_values
= encoder.transform(test_labels) print("\nLabels
=",test_labels)
print("Encoded values =", list(encoded_values))
encoded_values = [3,0,4,1]
decoded_list =
encoder.inverse_transform(encoded_values)
```

We can get the list of encoded values with the help of following python script:

```
print("\nEncoded values =", encoded_values)
print("\nDecoded labels =", list(decoded_list))
```

Output

```
Labels = ['green', 'red', 'black']
Encoded values = [1, 2, 0]
Encoded values = [3, 0, 4, 1]
Decoded labels = ['white', 'black', 'yellow',
'green']
```

Data Feature Selection

In the previous chapter, we have seen in detail how to preprocess and prepare data for machine learning. In this chapter,
let us understand in detail data feature selection and various
aspects involved in it.

Importance of Data Feature Selection

The performance of machine learning model is directly pro-
portional to the data features used to train it. The performance
of ML model will be affected negatively if the data features
provided to it are irrelevant. On the other hand, use of relevant
data features can increase the accuracy of your ML model
especially linear and logistic regression.

Now the question arise that what is automatic feature selection? It may be defined as the process with the help of which
we select those features in our data that are most relevant to
the output or prediction variable in which we are interested.
It is also called attribute selection.

The following are some of the benefits of automatic feature
selection before modeling the data:

- Performing feature selection before data modeling will reduce the over fitting.
- Performing feature selection before data modeling will increases the accuracy of ML model.
- Performing feature selection before data modeling will reduce the training time.

Feature Selection Techniques

The followings are automatic feature selection techniques that we can use to model ML data in Python:

Univariate Selection

This feature selection technique is very useful in selecting those features, with the help of statistical testing, having strongest relationship with the prediction variables. We can implement univariate feature selection technique with the help of **SelectKBest0**class of **scikit−learn** Python library.

Example:

In this example, we will use Pima Indians Diabetes dataset to select 4 of the attributes having best features with the help of chi−square statistical test.

```
from pandas import read_csv
from numpy import set_printoptions
from sklearn.feature_selectionimport SelectKBest
from sklearn.feature_selection import chi2 path =
r'C:\pima-indians-diabetes.csv'
```

```
names = ['preg', 'plas', 'pres', 'skin', 'test',
'mass', 'pedi', 'age',
'class']
dataframe = read_csv(path, names=names)
array = dataframe.values
```

Next, we will separate array into input and output components:

```
X = array[:,0:8] Y = array[:,8]
```

The following lines of code will select the best features from
dataset:

```
test = SelectKBest(score_func=chi2, k=4)
fit = test.fit(X,Y)
```

We can also summarize the data for output as per our choice.
Here, we are setting the precision to 2 and showing the 4 data
attributes with best features along with best score of each
attribute:

```
set_printoptions(precision=2)
print(fit.scores_)
featured_data = fit.transform(X)
print ("\nFeatured data:\n",featured_data[0:4])
```

Output

```
[ 111.52 1411.89   17.61   53.11 2175.57 127.67   5.39
181.3 ]
```

```
Featured data:
[[148.  0.   33.6  50.]
 [ 85.  0.   26.6  31.]
 [183.  0.   23.3  32.]
 [ 89.  94.  28.1  21.]]
```

Recursive Feature Elimination

As the name suggests, RFE (Recursive feature elimination) feature selection technique removes the attributes recursively and builds the model with remaining attributes. We can implement RFE feature selection technique with the help of **RFE** class of **scikit-learn** Python library.

Example

In this example, we will use RFE with logistic regression algorithm to select the best 3 attributes having the best features from Pima Indians Diabetes dataset to.

```
from pandas import read_csv
from sklearn.feature_selectionimport RFE
from sklearn.linear_model import LogisticRegression
path = r'C:\pima-indians-diabetes.csv'
names = ['preg', 'plas', 'pres', 'skin', 'test',
'mass', 'pedi', 'age',
'class']
dataframe = read_csv(path, names=names)
array = dataframe.values
```

Next, we will separate the array into its input and output components:

```
X = array[:,0:8] Y = array[:,8]
```

The following lines of code will select the best features from a dataset:

```
model = LogisticRegression()
rfe = RFE(model, 3) fit = rfe.fit(X, Y)
print("Number of Features: %d")print("Selected
Features: %s")
print("Feature Ranking: %s")
```

Output

```
Number of Features: 3
Selected Features: [ True False False False False
True True False] Feature Ranking: [1 2 3 5 6 1 1 4]
```

We can see in above output, RFE choose preg, mass and pedi as the first 3 best features. They are marked as 1 in the output.

Principal Component Analysis (PCA)

PCA, generally called data reduction technique, is very useful feature selection technique as it uses linear algebra to trans-form the dataset into a compressed form. We can implement PCA feature selection technique with the help of **PCA** class of **scikit-learn** Python library. We can select number of principal components in the output.

Example:

In this example, we will use PCA to select best 3 Principal components from Pima Indians Diabetes dataset.

```
from pandas import read_csv
from sklearn.decomposition import PCA
path = r'C:\pima-indians-diabetes.csv'
names = ['preg', 'plas', 'pres', 'skin', 'test',
'mass', 'pedi', 'age',
'class']
dataframe = read_csv(path, names=names)
array = dataframe.values
```

Next, we will separate array into input and output compo-nents:

```
X = array[:,0:8] Y = array[:,8]
```

The following lines of code will extract features from dataset:

```
pca = PCA(n_components=3)
fit = pca.fit(X)
print("Explained Variance: %s") %
fit.explained_variance_ratio_
print(fit.components_)
```

Output

```
Explained Variance: [ 0.88854663 0.06159078
0.02579012]
[[ -2.02176587e-03 9.78115765e-02 1.60930503e-02
6.07566861e-02
9.93110844e-01 1.40108085e-02
5.37167919e-04-3.56474430e-03]
```

```
[ 2.26488861e-02 9.72210040e-01 1.41909330e-01
-5.78614699e-02
-9.46266913e-02 4.69729766e-02 8.16804621e-04
1.40168181e-01]
[ -2.24649003e-02 1.43428710e-01 -9.22467192e-01
-3.07013055e-01
2.09773019e-02 -1.32444542e-01 -6.39983017e-04
-1.25454310e-01]]
```

We can observe from the above output that 3 Principal Components bear little resemblance to the source data.

Feature Importance

As the name suggests, feature importance technique is used to choose the importance features. It basically uses a trained supervised classifier to select features. We can implement this feature selection technique with the help of **ExtraTreeClassifier** class of **scikit-learn** Python library.

Example

In this example, we will use **ExtraTreeClassifier** to select features from Pima Indians Diabetes dataset.

```python
from pandas import read_csv
from sklearn.ensemble import ExtraTreesClassifier
path = r'C:\Desktop\pima-indians-diabetes.csv'
names = ['preg', 'plas', 'pres', 'skin', 'test',
'mass', 'pedi', 'age',
'class']
dataframe = read_csv(data, names=names)
```

```
array = dataframe.values
```

Next, we will separate array into input and output components:

```
X = array[:,0:8] Y = array[:,8]
```

The following lines of code will extract features from dataset:

```
model = ExtraTreesClassifier() model.fit(X, Y)
print(model.feature_importances_)
```

Output

```
[ 0.11070069 0.2213717 0.08824115 0.08068703
0.07281761 0.14548537 0.12654214 0.15415431]
```

From the output, we can observe that there are scores for each
attribute. The higher the score, higher is the importance of
that attribute.

Classifications

Classification may be defined as the process of predicting class or category from observed values or given data points. The categorized output can have the form such as "Black" or "White" or "spam" or "no spam".

Mathematically, classification is the task of approximating a mapping function (f) from input variables (X) to output variables (Y). It is basically belongs to the supervised machine learning in which targets are also provided along with the input data set.

An example of classification problem can be the spam detection in emails. There can be only two categories of output, "spam" and "no spam"; hence this is a binary type classification.

To implement this classification, we first need to train the classifier. For this example, "spam" and "no spam" emails would be used as the training data. After successfully train the classifier, it can be used to detect an unknown email.

Types of Learners in Classification

We have two types of learners in respective to classification problems:

Lazy Learners

As the name suggests, such kind of learners waits for the testing data to be appeared after storing the training data. Classification is done only after getting the testing data. They spend less time on training but more time on predicting. Examples of lazy learners are K- nearest neighbor and case-based reasoning.

Eager Learners

As opposite to lazy learners, eager learners construct classification model without waiting for the testing data to be appeared after storing the training data. They spend more time on training but less time on predicting. Examples of eager learners are Decision Trees, Naïve Bayes and Artificial Neural Networks (ANN).

Building a Classifier in Python

Scikit-learn, a Python library for machine learning can be used to build a classifier in Python. The steps for building a classifier in Python are as follows:

Step1: Importing necessary python package

For building a classifier using scikit-learn, we need to import it. We can import it by using following script:

```
import sklearn
```

Step2: Importing dataset

After importing necessary package, we need a dataset to build classification prediction model. We can import it from sklearn dataset or can use other one as per our requirement. We are going to use sklearn's Breast Cancer Wisconsin Diagnostic Database. We can import it with the help of following script:

```
from sklearn.datasets import load_breast_cancer
```

The following script will load the dataset;

```
data = load_breast_cancer()
```

We also need to organize the data and it can be done with the help of following scripts:

```
label_names = data['target_names']
labels = data['target']
feature_names = data['feature_names']
features = data['data']
```

The following command will print the name of the labels, **'malignant'** and **'benign'** in case of our database.

```
print(label_names)
```

The output of the above command is the names of the labels:

```
['malignant' 'benign']
```

These labels are mapped to binary values 0 and 1. **Malignant** cancer is represented by 0 and**Benign** cancer is represented by 1.

The feature names and feature values of these labels can be seen with the help of following commands:

```
print(feature_names[0])
```

The output of the above command is the names of the features for label 0 i.e. **Malignant** cancer:

```
mean radius
```

Similarly, names of the features for label can be produced as follows:

```
print(feature_names[1])
```

The output of the above command is the names of the features for label 1 i.e. **Benign** cancer:

```
mean texture
```

We can print the features for these labels with the help of

following command:

```python
print(features[0])
```

This will give the following output:

```
[1.799e+01 1.038e+01 1.228e+02 1.001e+03 1.184e-01 2.776e-01 3.001e-01
 1.471e-01 2.419e-01 7.871e-02 1.095e+00 9.053e-01 8.589e+00 1.534e+02
 6.399e-03 4.904e-02 5.373e-02 1.587e-02 3.003e-02 6.193e-03 2.538e+01
 1.733e+01 1.846e+02 2.019e+03 1.622e-01 6.656e-01 7.119e-01 2.654e-01
 4.601e-01 1.189e-01]
```

We can print the features for these labels with the help of following command:

```python
print(features[1])
```

This will give the following output:

```
[2.057e+01 1.777e+01 1.329e+02 1.326e+03 8.474e-02 7.864e-02 8.690e-02
 7.017e-02 1.812e-01 5.667e-02 5.435e-01 7.339e-01 3.398e+00 7.408e+01
 5.225e-03 1.308e-02 1.860e-02 1.340e-02 1.389e-02 3.532e-03 2.499e+01
 2.341e+01 1.588e+02 1.956e+03 1.238e-01 1.866e-01 2.416e-01 1.860e-01
 2.750e-01 8.902e-02]
```

Step 3: Organizing data into training & testing sets

As we need to test our model on unseen data, we will divide our dataset into two parts: a training set and a test set. We can use **train_test_split()** function of **sklearn** python package to split the data into sets. The following command will import the function:

```
from sklearn.model_selection import train_test_split
```

Now, next command will split the data into training & testing data. In this example, we are using taking 40 percent of the data for testing purpose and 60 percent of the data for training purpose:

```
train, test, train_labels, test_labels =
train_test_split(features, labels, test_size = 0.40,
random_state = 42)
```

Step 4 – Model evaluation

After dividing the data into training and testing we need to build the model. We will be using **Naïve Bayes** algorithm for this purpose. The following commands will import the **GaussianNB** module:

```
from sklearn.naive_bayes import GaussianNB
```

Now, initialize the model as follows:

```
gnb = GaussianNB()
```

Next, with the help of following command we can train the model:

```
model = gnb.fit(train, train_labels)
```

Now, for evaluation purpose we need to make predictions. It

can be done by using **predict()** function as follows:

```
preds = gnb.predict(test)
print(preds)
```

This will give the following output:

```
[1 0 0 1 1 0 0 0 1 1 1 0 1 0 1 0 1 1 1 0 1 1 0 1 1 1 1 1 1 0 1 1 1 1 1 1 0
 1 0 1 1 0 1 1 1 1 1 1 1 1 0 0 1 1 1 1 1 0 0 1 1 0 0 1 1 1 0 0 1 1 0 0 1 0
 1 1 1 1 1 1 0 1 1 0 0 0 0 0 1 1 1 1 1 1 1 0 0 1 0 0 1 0 0 1 1 1 0 1 1 0
 1 1 0 0 0 1 1 1 0 0 1 1 0 1 0 0 1 1 0 0 0 1 1 1 0 1 1 0 0 1 0 1 1 0 1 0 0
 1 1 1 1 1 1 0 0 1 1 1 1 1 1 1 1 1 1 1 0 1 1 1 0 1 1 0 1 1 1 1 1 1 0 0
 0 1 1 0 1 0 1 1 1 1 0 1 1 0 1 1 1 0 1 0 0 1 1 1 1 1 1 1 1 0 1 1 1 1 1 0 1
 0 0 1 1 0 1]
```

The above series of 0s and 1s in output are the predicted values
for the **Malignant** and **Benign** tumor classes.

Step 5- Finding accuracy

We can find the accuracy of the model build in previous step by
comparing the two arrays namely **test_labels** and **preds.**We
will be using the **accuracy_score()** function to determine the
accuracy.

```
fromsklearn.metrics import accuracy_score
print(accuracy_score(test_labels,preds))
0.951754385965
```

The above output shows that **NaïveBayes** classifier is 95.17%
accurate.

Classification Evaluation Metrics

The job is not done even if you have finished implementation of your Machine Learning application or model. We must have to find out how effective our model is? There can be different evaluation metrics, but we must choose it carefully because the choice of metrics influences how the performance of a machine learning algorithm is measured and compared.

The following are some of the important classification evaluation metrics among which you can choose based upon your dataset and kind of problem:

Confusion Matrix

It is the easiest way to measure the performance of a classification problem where the output can be of two or more type of classes. A confusion matrix is nothing but a table with two dimensions viz. "Actual" and "Predicted" and furthermore, both the dimensions have "True Positives (TP)", "True Negatives (TN)", "False Positives (FP)", "False Negatives (FN)" as shown below:

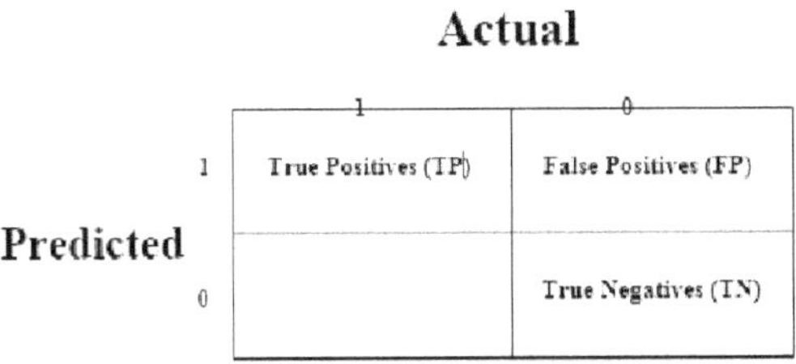

The explanation of the terms associated with confusion matrix are as follows:

- **True Positives (TP):** It is the case when both actual class & predicted class of data point is 1.
- **True Negatives (TN):** It is the case when both actual class & predicted class of data point is 0.
- **False Positives (FP):** It is the case when actual class of data point is 0 &predicted class of data point is 1.
- **False Negatives (FN):** It is the case when actual class of data point is 1 & predicted class of data point is 0.

We can find the confusion matrix with the help of **confusion_matrix()** function of **sklearn**. With the help of the following script, we can find the confusion matrix of above built binary classifier:

```
from sklearn.metrics import confusion_matrix
```

Output

```
[[ 73   7]
 [  4 144]]
```

Accuracy

It may be defined as the number of correct predictions made by our ML model. We can easily calculate it by confusion matrix with the help of following formula:

$$Accuracy = \frac{TP + TN}{TP + FP + FN + TN}$$

For above built binary classifier, TP + TN = 73+144 = 217 and TP+FP+FN+TN = 73+7+4+144=228.

Hence, Accuracy = 217/228 = 0.951754385965 which is same as we have calculated after creating our binary classifier.

Precision

Precision, used in document retrievals, may be defined as the number of correct documents returned by our ML model. We can easily calculate it by confusion matrix with the help of following formula:

$$Precision = \frac{TP}{TP + FP}$$

For the above built binary classifier, TP = 73 and TP+FP = 73+7 = 80. Hence, Precision = 73/80 = 0.915

Recall or Sensitivity

Recall may be defined as the number of positives returned by our ML model. We can easily calculate it by confusion matrix with the help of following formula:

$$Recall = \frac{TP}{TP + FN}$$

For above built binary classifier, TP = 73 and TP+FN = 73+4 = 77. Hence, Precision = 73/77 = 0.94805

Specificity

Specificity, in contrast to recall, may be defined as the number of negatives returned by our ML model. We can easily calculate it by confusion matrix with the help of following formula:

$$Specificity = \frac{TN}{TN + FP}$$

For the above built binary classifier, TN = 144 and TN+FP = 144+7 = 151. Hence, Precision = 144/151 = 0.95364

Various ML Classification Algorithms

The followings are some important ML classification algorithms:

- Logistic Regression
- Support Vector Machine (SVM)
- Decision Tree
- Naïve Bayes
- Random Forest

We will be discussing all these classification algorithms in detail in further chapters.

Applications

Some of the most important applications of classification algorithms are as follows:

- Speech Recognition
- Handwriting Recognition
- Biometric Identification
- Document Classification

Logistic Regression

Logistic regression is a supervised learning classification algorithm used to predict the probability of a target variable. The nature of target or dependent variable is dichotomous, which means there would be only two possible classes.

In simple words, the dependent variable is binary in nature having data coded as either 1 (stands for success/yes) or 0 (stands for failure/no).

Mathematically, a logistic regression model predicts $P(Y=1)$ as a function of X. It is one of the simplest ML algorithms that can be used for various classification problems such as spam detection, Diabetes prediction, cancer detection etc.

Types of Logistic Regression

Generally, logistic regression means binary logistic regression having binary target variables, but there can be two more categories of target variables that can be predicted by it. Based on those number of categories, Logistic regression can be divided into following types:

Binary or Binomial

In such a kind of classification, a dependent variable will have only two possible types either 1 and 0. For example, these variables may represent success or failure, yes or no, win or loss etc.

Multinomial

In such a kind of classification, dependent variable can have 3 or more possible **unordered** types or the types having no quantitative significance. For example, these variables may represent "Type A" or "Type B" or "Type C".

Ordinal

In such a kind of classification, dependent variable can have 3 or more possible **ordered** types or the types having a quantitative significance. For example, these variables may represent "poor" or "good", "very good", "Excellent" and each category can have the scores like 0,1,2,3.

Logistic Regression Assumptions

Before diving into the implementation of logistic regression, we must be aware of the following assumptions about the same:

- In case of binary logistic regression, the target variables must be binary always and the desired outcome is represented by the factor level 1.

- There should not be any multi-collinearity in the model, which means the independent variables must be independent of each other.
- We must include meaningful variables in our model.
- We should choose a large sample size for logistic regression.

Binary Logistic Regression model

The simplest form of logistic regression is binary or binomial logistic regression in which the target or dependent variable can have only 2 possible types either 1 or 0. It allows us to model a relationship between multiple predictor variables and a binary/binomial target variable. In case of logistic regression, the linear function is basically used as an input to another function such as in the following relation:

$$h_\theta(x) = g(\theta^T x) \, where \, 0 \leq h_\theta \leq 1$$

Here, is the logistic or sigmoid function which can be given as follows:

$$g(z) = \frac{1}{1+e^{-z}} \, where z = \theta^T x$$

To sigmoid curve can be represented with the help of following graph. We can see the values of y-axis lie between 0 and 1 and crosses the axis at 0.5.

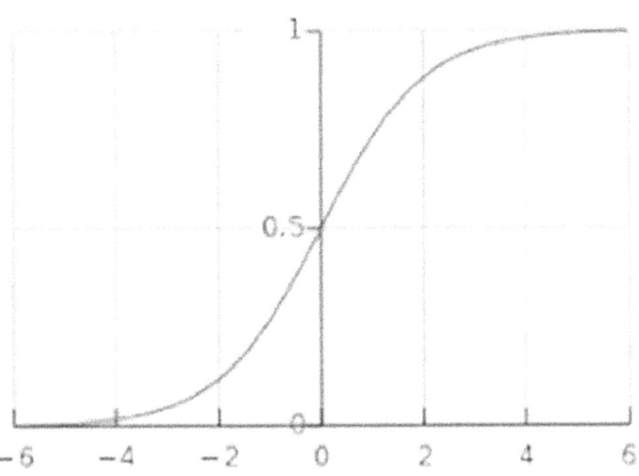

The classes can be divided into positive or negative. The output comes under the probability of positive class if it lies between 0 and 1. For our implementation, we are interpreting the output of hypothesis function as positive if it is ≥ 0.5, otherwise negative. We also need to define a loss function to measure how well the algorithm performs using the weights on functions, represented by theta as follows:

$$h = g(X\theta)$$

$$J(\theta) = \frac{1}{m} \cdot \left(-y^T log(h) - (1-y)^T log(1-h)\right)$$

Now, after defining the loss function our prime goal is to minimize the loss function. It can be done with the help of fitting the weights which means by increasing or decreasing the weights. With the help of derivatives of the loss function w.r.t each weight, we would be able to know what parameters should have high weight and what should have smaller weight.

The following gradient descent equation tells us how loss would change if we modified the parameters:

$$\frac{\delta J(\theta)}{\delta \theta_j} = \frac{1}{m} X^T \left(g(X\theta) - y\right)$$

Implementation in Python

Now we will implement the above concept of binomial logistic regression in Python. For this purpose, we are using a multivariate flower dataset named 'iris' which have 3 classes of 50 instances each, but we will be using the first two feature columns. Every class represents a type of iris flower.

First, we need to import the necessary libraries as follows:

```
import numpy as np
import matplotlib.pyplot as plt import seaborn as sns
from sklearn import datasets
```

Next, load the iris dataset as follows:

```
iris = datasets.load_iris() X = iris.data[:, :2]
y = (iris.target != 0) * 1
```

We can plot our training data s follows:

```
plt.figure(figsize=(6, 6))
plt.scatter(X[y == 0][:, 0], X[y == 0][:, 1], color='g', label='0')
plt.scatter(X[y == 1][:, 0], X[y == 1][:, 1], color='y', label='1')
plt.legend();
```

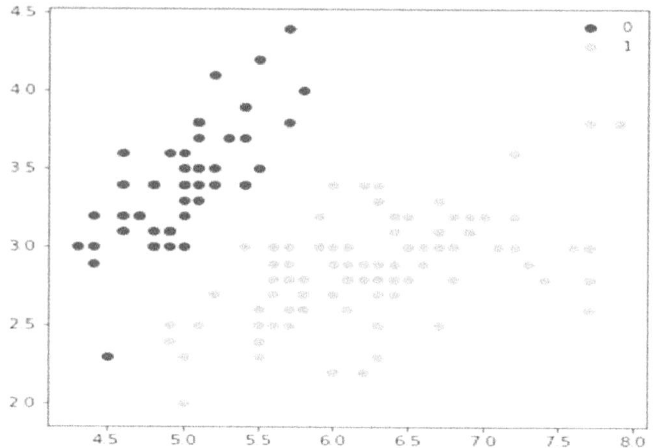

Next, we will define sigmoid function, loss function and gradient descend as follows:

```python
class LogisticRegression:
def  init (self, lr=0.01, num_iter=100000,
fit_intercept=True, verbose=False):
self.lr = lr self.num_iter = num_iter
self.fit_intercept = fit_intercept self.verbose =
verbose
def  add_intercept(self, X):
intercept = np.ones((X.shape[0], 1))
return np.concatenate((intercept, X), axis=1)
def  sigmoid(self, z):
return 1 / (1 + np.exp(-z))
def  loss(self, h, y):
return (-y * np.log(h) - (1 - y) * np.log(1 -
h)).mean()
def fit(self, X, y):
if self.fit_intercept:
X = self. add_intercept(X)
```

Now, initialize the weights as follows:

```python
self.theta = np.zeros(X.shape[1])
for i in range(self.num_iter):
z = np.dot(X, self.theta)
h = self. sigmoid(z)
gradient = np.dot(X.T, (h - y)) / y.size self.theta
-= self.lr * gradient
z = np.dot(X, self.theta)
h = self. sigmoid(z)
loss = self. loss(h, y)
if(self.verbose ==True and i % 10000 == 0):
print(f'loss: {loss} \t')
```

With the help of the following script, we can predict the output probabilities:

```python
def predict_prob(self, X):
if self.fit_intercept:
X = self. add_intercept(X)
return self. sigmoid(np.dot(X, self.theta))
def predict(self, X):
return self.predict_prob(X).round()
```

Next, we can evaluate the model and plot it as follows:

```python
model = LogisticRegression(lr=0.1, num_iter=300000)
preds = model.predict(X) (preds == y).mean()
plt.figure(figsize=(10, 6))
plt.scatter(X[y == 0][:, 0], X[y == 0][:, 1],
color='g', label='0') plt.scatter(X[y == 1][:, 0],
X[y == 1][:, 1], color='y', label='1') plt.legend()
x1_min, x1_max = X[:,0].min(),X[:,0].max(), x2_min,
x2_max = X[:,1].min(),X[:,1].max(),
xx1, xx2 = np.meshgrid(np.linspace(x1_min, x1_max),
```

```
np.linspace(x2_min, x2_max))
grid = np.c_[xx1.ravel(), xx2.ravel()]
probs = model.predict_prob(grid).reshape(xx1.shape)
plt.contour(xx1, xx2, probs, [0.5], linewidths=1,
colors='red');
```

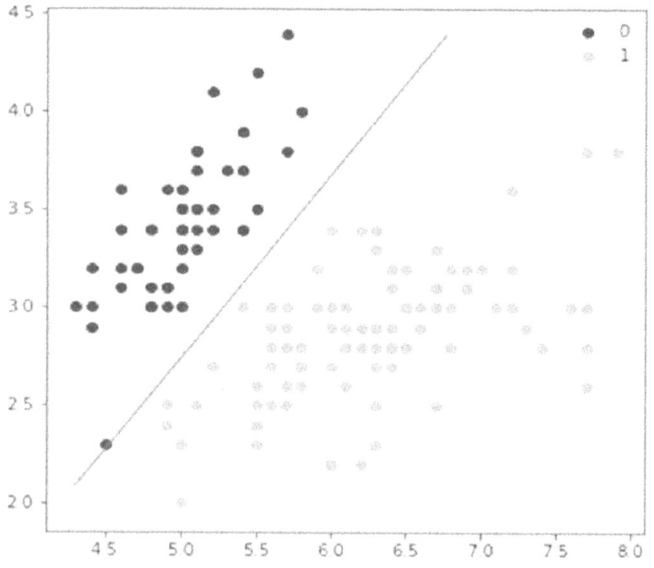

Multinomial Logistic Regression Model

Another useful form of logistic regression is multinomial logistic regression in which the target or dependent variable can have 3 or more possible **unordered** types i.e. the types having no quantitative significance.

Implementation in Python

Now we will implement the above concept of multinomial logistic regression in Python. For this purpose, we are using a dataset from sklearn named *digit*.

First, we need to import the necessary libraries as follows:

```
Import sklearn
from sklearn import datasets
from sklearn import linear_model fromsklearn import
metrics
from sklearn.model_selection import train_test_split
```

Next, we need to load digit dataset:

```
digits = datasets.load_digits()
```

Now, define the feature matrix(X) and response vector(y)as follows:

```
X = digits.data
y = digits.target
```

With the help of next line of code, we can split X and y into training and testing sets:

```
X_train, X_test, y_train, y_test =
train_test_split(X, y,
test_size=0.4, random_state=
1)
```

Now create an object of logistic regression as follows:

```
digreg = linear_model.LogisticRegression()
```

Now, we need to train the model by using the training sets as follows:

```
digreg.fit(X_train, y_train)
```

Next, make the predictions on testing set as follows:

```
y_pred = digreg.predict(X_test)
```

Next print the accuracy of the model as follows:

```
print("Accuracy of Logistic Regression model is:",
metrics.accuracy_score(y_test, y_pred)*100)
```

Output

```
Accuracy of Logistic Regression model is:
95.6884561891516
```

From the above output we can see the accuracy of our model is around 96 percent.

Support Vector Machine (SVM)

Support vector machines (SVMs) are powerful yet flexible supervised machine learning algorithms which are used both for classification and regression. But generally, they are used in classification problems. In 1960s, SVMs were first introduced but later they got refined in 1990. SVMs have their unique way of implementation as compared to other machine learning algorithms. Lately, they are extremely popular because of their ability to handle multiple continuous and categorical variables.

Working of SVM

An SVM model is basically a representation of different classes in a hyperplane in multidimensional space. The hyperplane will be generated in an iterative manner by SVM so that the error can be minimized. The goal of SVM is to divide the datasets into classes to find a maximum marginal hyperplane (MMH).

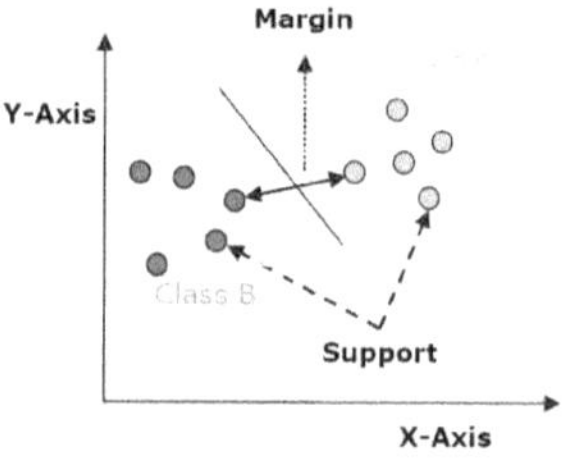

The followings are important concepts in SVM:

- **Support Vectors:** Datapoints that are closest to the hyperplane is called support vectors. Separating line will be
defined with the help of these data points.
- **Hyperplane:** As we can see in the above diagram, it is a
decision plane or space which is divided between a set of
objects having different classes.
- **Margin:** It may be defined as the gap between two lines
on the closet data points of different classes. It can be
calculated as the perpendicular distance from the line to
the support vectors. Large margin is considered as a good
margin and small margin is considered as a bad margin.

The main goal of SVM is to divide the datasets into classes to
find a maximum marginal hyperplane (MMH) and it can be
done in the following two steps:

- First, SVM will generate hyperplanes iteratively that seg-
regates the classes in best way.
- Then, it will choose the hyperplane that separates the
classes correctly.

Implementing SVM in Python

For implementing SVM in Python we will start with the standard libraries import as follows:

```python
import numpy as np
import matplotlib.pyplot as plt
from scipy import stats
import seaborn as sns; sns.set()
```

Next, we are creating a sample dataset, having linearly separable data, from sklearn.dataset.sample_generator for classification using SVM:

```python
from sklearn.datasets.samples_generator import
make_blobs
X, y = make_blobs(n_samples=100, centers=2,
         random_state=0, cluster_std=0.50)
plt.scatter(X[:, 0], X[:, 1], c=y, s=50,
cmap='summer');
```

The following would be the output after generating sample dataset having 100 samples and 2 clusters:

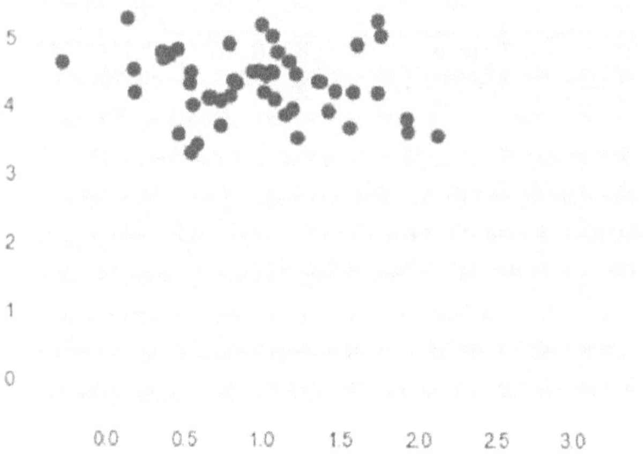

We know that SVM supports discriminative classification. it divides the classes from each other by simply finding a line in case of two dimensions or manifold in case of multiple dimensions. It is implemented on the above dataset as follows:

```
xfit = np.linspace(-1, 3.5)
plt.scatter(X[:, 0], X[:, 1], c=y, s=50,
cmap='summer')
plt.plot([0.6], [2.1], 'x', color='black',
markeredgewidth=4, markersize=12)
for m, b in [(1, 0.65), (0.5, 1.6), (-0.2, 2.9)]:
plt.plot(xfit, m * xfit + b, '-k')
plt.xlim(-1, 3.5);
```

The output is as follows:

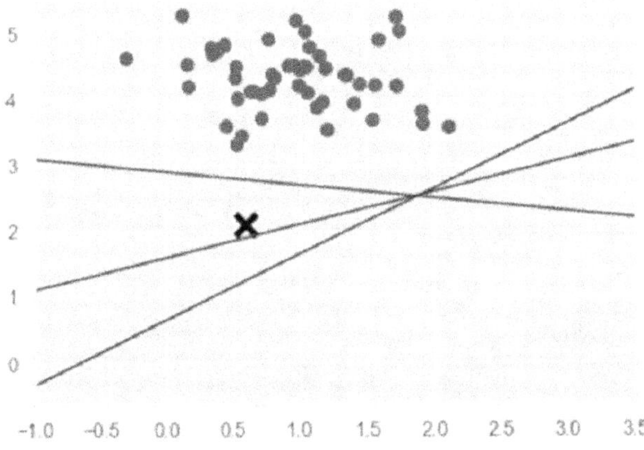

We can see from the above output that there are three different separators that perfectly discriminate the above samples.

As discussed, the main goal of SVM is to divide the datasets into classes to find a maximum marginal hyperplane (MMH) hence rather than drawing a zero line between classes we can draw around each line a margin of some width up to the nearest point. It can be done as follows:

```python
xfit = np.linspace(-1, 3.5)
plt.scatter(X[:, 0], X[:, 1], c=y, s=50,
cmap='summer')
for m, b, d in [(1, 0.65, 0.33),(0.5, 1.6,
0.55),(-0.2, 2.9, 0.2)]:
yfit= m * xfit + b plt.plot(xfit, yfit, '-k')
plt.fill_between(xfit, yfit - d, yfit + d,
edgecolor='none', color='#AAAAAA', alpha=0.4)
plt.xlim(-1, 3.5);
```

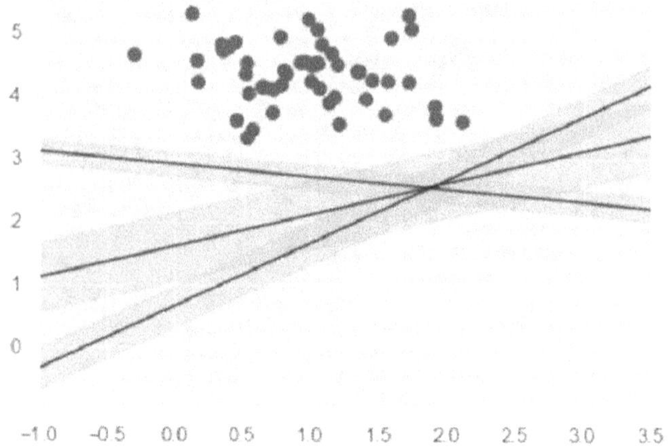

From the above image in output, we can easily observe the "margins" within the discriminative classifiers. SVM will choose the line that maximizes the margin.

Next, we will use Scikit-Learn's support vector classifier to train an SVM model on this data. Here, we are using linear kernel to fit SVM as follows:

```
from sklearn.svm import SVC # "Support vector
classifier" model = SVC(kernel='linear', C=1E10)
model.fit(X, y)
```

The output is as follows:

```
SVC(C=10000000000.0, cache_size=200,
class_weight=None, coef0=0.0,
decision_function_shape='ovr', degree=3,
gamma='auto_deprecated', kernel='linear',
```

```
max_iter=-1, probability=False, random_state=None,
shrinking=True, tol=0.001, verbose=False)
```

Now, for a better understanding, the following will plot the decision functions for 2D SVC:

```
def decision_function(model, ax=None,
plot_support=True):
if ax is None:
ax = plt.gca()
xlim = ax.get_xlim()
ylim = ax.get_ylim()
```

For evaluating model, we need to create grid as follows:

```
x = np.linspace(xlim[0], xlim[1], 30)
y = np.linspace(ylim[0], ylim[1], 30)
Y, X = np.meshgrid(y, x)
xy = np.vstack([X.ravel(),Y.ravel()]).T
P = model.decision_function(xy).reshape(X.shape)
```

Next, we need to plot decision boundaries and margins as follows:

```
ax.contour(X, Y, P, colors='k',
levels=[-1, 0, 1], alpha=0.5, linestyles=['--', '-',
'--'])
```

Now, similarly plot the support vectors as follows:

```
if plot_support:
ax.scatter(model.support_vectors_[:, 0],
model.support_vectors_[:, 1],
s=300, linewidth=1, facecolors='none');
ax.set_xlim(xlim)
ax.set_ylim(ylim)
```

Now, use this function to fit our models as follows:

```
plt.scatter(X[:, 0], X[:, 1], c=y, s=50,
cmap='summer')
decision_function(model);
```

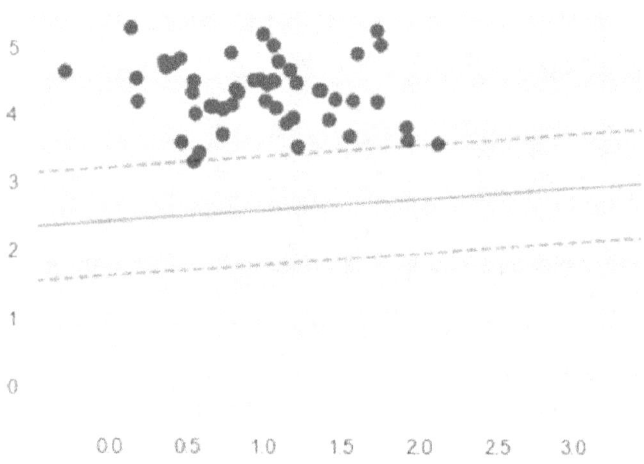

We can observe from the above output that an SVMclassifier fit to the data with margins i.e. dashed lines and support vectors, the pivotal elements of this fit, touching the dashed line. These support vector points are stored in the **support_vectors_**

attribute of the classifier as follows:

```
model.support_vectors_
```

The output is as follows:

```
array([[0.5323772 , 3.31338909], [2.11114739,
3.57660449],
[1.46870582, 1.86947425]])
```

SVM Kernels

In practice, SVM algorithm is implemented with kernel that transforms an input data space into the required form. SVM uses a technique called the kernel trick in which kernel takes a low dimensional input space and transforms it into a higher dimensional space. In simple words, kernel converts non-separable problems into separable problems by adding more dimensions to it. It makes SVM more powerful, flexible and accurate. The following are some of the types of kernels used by SVM:

Linear Kernel

It can be used as a dot product between any two observations. The formula of linear kernel is as below:

```
k(x,xi) = sum(x*xi)
```

From the above formula, we can see that the product between

two vectors say & is the sum of the multiplication of each pair of input values.

Polynomial Kernel

It is more generalized form of linear kernel and distinguish curved or nonlinear input space. Following is the formula for polynomial kernel:

```
K(x, xi) = 1 + sum(x * xi)^d
```

Here d is the degree of polynomial, which we need to specify manually in the learning algorithm.

Radial Basis Function (RBF) Kernel

RBF kernel, mostly used in SVM classification, maps input space in indefinite dimensional space. Following formula explains it mathematically:

```
K(x,xi) = exp(-gamma * sum((x - xi^2))
```

Here, *gamma* ranges from 0 to 1. We need to manually specify it in the learning algorithm. A good default value of *gamma* is 0.1.

As we implemented SVM for linearly separable data, we can implement it in Python for the data that is not linearly separable. It can be done by using kernels.

Example

The following is an example for creating an SVM classifier by using kernels. We will be using **iris** dataset from **scikit-learn**:

We will start by importing following packages:

```
import pandas as pd import numpy as np
from sklearn import svm, datasets
import matplotlib.pyplot as plt
Now, we need to load the input data:
iris = datasets.load_iris()
```

From this dataset, we are taking first two features as follows:

```
X = iris.data[:, :2]
y = iris.target
```

Next, we will plot the SVM boundaries with original data as follows:

```
x_min, x_max = X[:, 0].min() - 1, X[:, 0].max() + 1
y_min, y_max = X[:,1].min() - 1, X[:, 1].max() + 1 h
= (x_max / x_min)/100
xx, yy = np.meshgrid(np.arange(x_min, x_max, h),
np.arange(y_min, y_max, h))
X_plot = np.c_[xx.ravel(), yy.ravel()]
```

Now, we need to provide the value of regularization parameter as follows:

```
C = 1.0
Next, SVM classifier object can be created as
follows: Svc_classifier = svm.SVC(kernel='linear',
C=C).fit(X, y)
Z = svc_classifier.predict(X_plot) Z =
Z.reshape(xx.shape) plt.figure(figsize=(15, 5))
plt.subplot(121)
plt.contourf(xx, yy, Z, cmap=plt.cm.tab10,
alpha=0.3) plt.scatter(X[:, 0], X[:, 1], c=y,
cmap=plt.cm.Set1) plt.xlabel('Sepal length')
plt.ylabel('Sepal width')
plt.xlim(xx.min(), xx.max())
plt.title('Support Vector Classifier with linear
kernel')
```

Output

Text(0.5, 1.0, 'Support Vector Classifier with linear kernel')

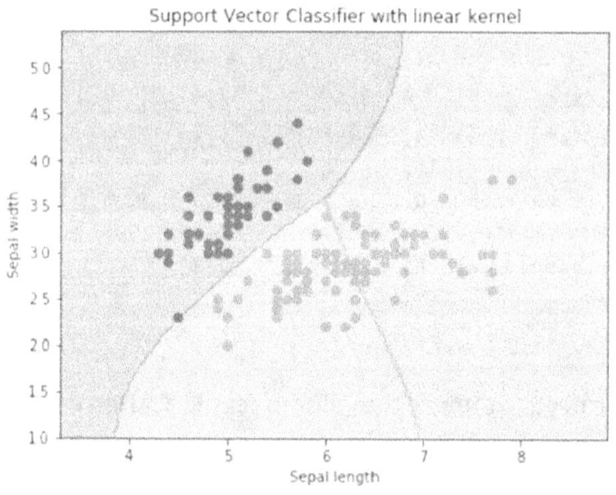

For creating SVM classifier with **rbf** kernel, we can change the kernel to **rbf** as follows:

```python
Svc_classifier = svm.SVC(kernel='rbf', gamma
='auto',C=C).fit(X, y) Z =
svc_classifier.predict(X_plot)
Z = Z.reshape(xx.shape)
plt.figure(figsize=(15, 5))
plt.subplot(121)
plt.contourf(xx, yy, Z, cmap=plt.cm.tab10,
alpha=0.3) plt.scatter(X[:, 0], X[:, 1], c=y,
cmap=plt.cm.Set1) plt.xlabel('Sepal length')
plt.ylabel('Sepal width')
plt.xlim(xx.min(), xx.max())
plt.title('Support Vector Classifier with rbf
kernel')
```

Output

```
Text(0.5, 1.0, 'Support Vector Classifier with rbf
kernel')
```

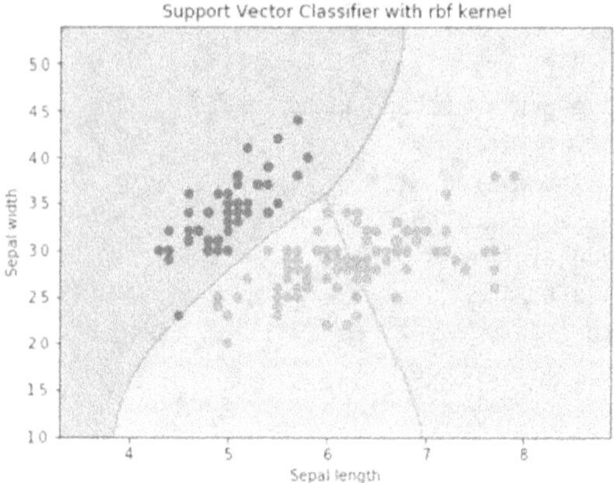

We put the value of gamma to 'auto' but you can provide its value between 0 to 1 also.

Pros and Cons of SVM Classifiers

Pros of SVM classifiers

SVM classifiers offers great accuracy and work well with high dimensional space. SVM classifiers basically use a subset of training points hence in result uses very less memory.

Cons of SVM classifiers

They have high training time hence in practice not suitable for large datasets. Another disadvantage is that SVM classifiers do not work well with overlapping classes.

Decision Tree

In general, Decision tree analysis is a predictive modeling tool that can be applied across many areas. Decision trees can be constructed by an algorithmic approach that can split the dataset in different ways based on different conditions. Decisions tress are the most powerful algorithms that falls under the category of supervised algorithms.

They can be used for both classification and regression tasks. The two main entities of a tree are decision nodes, where the data is split and leaves, where we got outcome. The example of a binary tree for predicting whether a person is fit or unfit providing various information like age, eating habits and exercise habits, is given below:

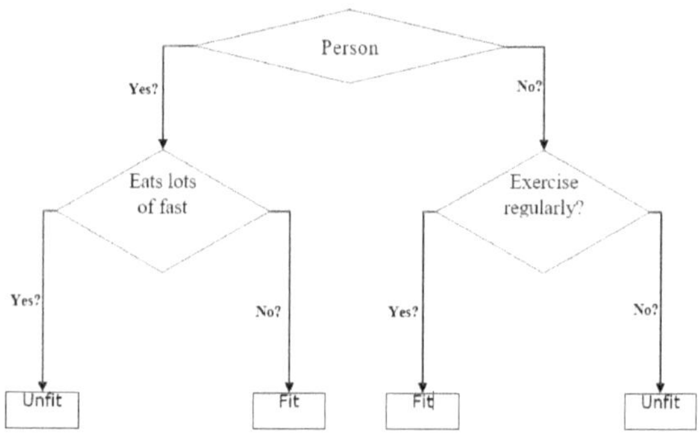

In the above decision tree, the question are decision nodes and final outcomes are leaves. We have the following two types of decision trees:

- **Classification decision trees:** In this kind of decision trees, the decision variable is categorical. The above decision tree is an example of classification decision tree.
- **Regression decision trees:** In this kind of decision trees, the decision variable is continuous.

Implementing Decision Tree Algorithm

Gini Index

It is the name of the cost function that is used to evaluate the binary splits in the dataset and works with the categorial target variable "Success" or "Failure".

Higher the value of Gini index, higher the homogeneity. A perfect Gini index value is 0 and worst is 0.5 (for 2 class problem). Gini index for a split can be calculated with the help of following steps:

- First, calculate Gini index for sub-nodes by using the formula p^2+q^2 , which is the sum of the square of probability for success and failure.
- Next, calculate Gini index for split using weighted Gini score of each node of that split.

Classification and Regression Tree (CART) algorithm uses Gini method to generate binary splits.

Split Creation

A split is basically including an attribute in the dataset and a value. We can create a split in dataset with the help of following three parts:

- **Part 1: Calculating Gini Score:** We have just discussed this part in the previous section.
- **Part 2: Splitting a dataset:** It may be defined as separating a dataset into two lists of rows having index of an attribute and a split value of that attribute. After getting the two groups - right and left, from the dataset, we can calculate the value of split by using Gini score calculated in first part. Split value will decide in which group the attribute will reside.
- **Part 3: Evaluating all splits:** Next part after finding Gini score and splitting dataset is the evaluation of all splits. For this purpose, first, we must check every value associated with each attribute as a candidate split. Then we need to find the best possible split by evaluating the

cost of the split. The best split will be used as a node in the decision tree.

Building a Tree

As we know that a tree has root node and terminal nodes. After creating the root node, we can build the tree by following two parts:

Part 1: Terminal node creation

While creating terminal nodes of decision tree, one important point is to decide when to stop growing tree or creating further terminal nodes. It can be done by using two criteria namely maximum tree depth and minimum node records as follows:

- **Maximum Tree Depth:** As name suggests, this is the maximum number of the nodes in a tree after root node. We must stop adding terminal nodes once a tree reached at maximum depth i.e. once a tree got maximum number of terminal nodes.
- **Minimum Node Records:** It may be defined as the minimum number of training patterns that a given node is responsible for. We must stop adding terminal nodes once tree reached at these minimum node records or below this minimum.

Terminal node is used to make a final prediction.

Part 2: Recursive Splitting

As we understood about when to create terminal nodes, now we can start building our tree. Recursive splitting is a method to build the tree. In this method, once a node is created, we can create the child nodes (nodes added to an existing node) recursively on each group of data, generated by splitting the dataset, by calling the same function again and again.

Prediction

After building a decision tree, we need to make a prediction about it. Basically, prediction involves navigating the decision tree with the specifically provided row of data.

We can make a prediction with the help of recursive function, as did above. The same prediction routine is called again with the left or the child right nodes.

Assumptions

The following are some of the assumptions we make while creating decision tree:

- While preparing decision trees, the training set is as root node.
- Decision tree classifier prefers the features values to be categorical. In case if you want to use continuous values then they must be done discretized prior to model building.
- Based on the attribute's values, the records are recursively distributed.
- Statistical approach will be used to place attributes at any

node position i.e.as root node or internal node.

Implementation in Python

Example

In the following example, we are going to implement Decision Tree classifier on Pima Indian Diabetes:

First, start with importing necessary python packages:

```python
import pandas as pd
from sklearn.tree import DecisionTreeClassifier
from sklearn.model_selectionimport train_test_split
```

Next, download the iris dataset from its web link as follows:

```python
col_names = ['pregnant', 'glucose', 'bp', 'skin',
'insulin', 'bmi', 'pedigree',
'age', 'label']
pima = pd.read_csv(r"C:\pima-indians-diabetes.csv",
header=None, names=col_names)
pima.head()
```

	pregnant	glucose	bp	skin	insulin	bmi	pedigree	age	label
0	6	148	72	35	0	33.6	0.627	50	1
1	1	85	66	29	0	26.6	0.351	31	0
2	8	183	64	0	0	23.3	0.672	32	1
3	1	89	66	23	94	28.1	0.167	21	0
4	0	137	40	35	168	43.1	2.288	33	1

Now, split the dataset into features and target variable as follows:

```python
feature_cols = ['pregnant', 'insulin', 'bmi',
'age','glucose','bp','pedigree'] X =
pima[feature_cols] # Features
y = pima.label # Target variable
```

Next, we will divide the data into train and test split. The following code will split the dataset into 70% training data and 30% of testing data:

```python
X_train, X_test, y_train, y_test =
train_test_split(X, y, test_size=0.3, random_state=1)
```

Next, train the model with the help of **DecisionTreeClassifier** class of **sklearn**as follows:

```python
clf = DecisionTreeClassifier()
clf = clf.fit(X_train,y_train)
```

At last we need to make prediction. It can be done with the help of following script:

```python
y_pred = clf.predict(X_test)
```

Next, we can get the accuracy score, confusion matrix and classification report as follows:

```python
from sklearn.metrics import classification_report,
confusion_matrix, accuracy_score
result = confusion_matrix(y_test, y_pred)
print("Confusion Matrix:")
print(result)
result1 = classification_report(y_test, y_pred)
print("Classification Report:",)
print (result1)
result2 = accuracy_score(y_test,y_pred)
print("Accuracy:",result2)
```

Output

```
Confusion Matrix:
[[116   30]
 [ 46   39]]
Classification Report:
              precision    recall  f1-score   support

           0       0.72      0.79      0.75       146
           1       0.57      0.46      0.51        85


   micro avg       0.67      0.67      0.67       231
   macro avg       0.64      0.63      0.63       231
weighted avg       0.66      0.67      0.66       231


Accuracy: 0.670995670995671
```

Visualizing Decision Tree

The above decision tree can be visualized with the help of
following code:

```python
from sklearn.tree import export_graphviz
fromsklearn.externals.six import StringIO
fromIPython.display import Image
import pydotplus
dot_data = StringIO()
export_graphviz(clf, out_file=dot_data, filled=True,
rounded=True,
special_characters=True,feature_names =
feature_cols,class_names=['0','1'])
graph =
pydotplus.graph_from_dot_data(dot_data.getvalue())
graph.write_png('Pima_diabetes_Tree.png')
Image(graph.create_png())
```

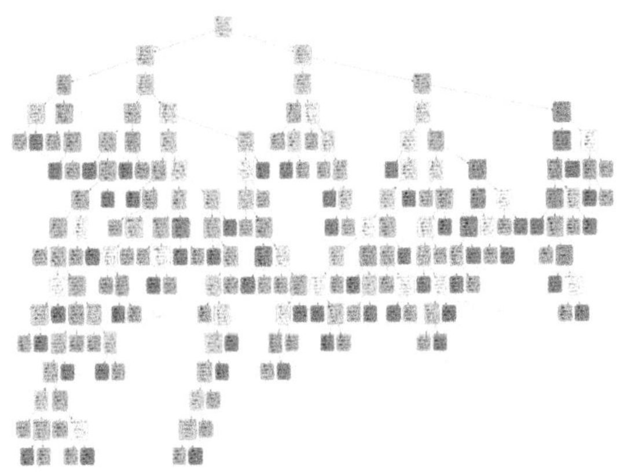

Naïve Bayes

Naïve Bayes algorithms is a classification technique based on applying Bayes' theorem with a strong assumption that all the predictors are independent to each other. In simple words, the assumption is that the presence of a feature in a class is independent to the presence of any other feature in the same class. For example, a phone may be considered as smart if it is having touch screen, internet facility, good camera etc. Though all these features are dependent on each other, they contribute independently to the probability of that the phone is a smart phone.

Building model using Naïve Bayes in Python

Python library, Scikit learn is the most useful library that helps us to build a Naïve Bayes model in Python. We have the following three types of Naïve Bayes model under Scikit learn Python library:

Gaussian Naïve Bayes

It is the simplest Naïve Bayes classifier having the assumption that the data from each label is drawn from a simple Gaussian distribution.

Multinomial Naïve Bayes

Another useful Naïve Bayes classifier is Multinomial Naïve Bayes in which the features are assumed to be drawn from a simple Multinomial distribution. Such kind of Naïve Bayes are most appropriate for the features that represents discrete counts.

Bernoulli Naïve Bayes

Another important model is Bernoulli Naïve Bayes in which features are assumed to be binary (0s and 1s). Text classification with 'bag of words' model can be an application of Bernoulli Naïve Bayes.

Example

Depending on our data set, we can choose any of the Naïve Bayes model explained above. Here, we are implementing Gaussian Naïve Bayes model in Python:

We will start with required imports as follows:

```
import numpy as np
import matplotlib.pyplot as plt import seaborn as
sns; sns.set()
```

Now, by using **make_blobs()** function of **Scikit learn,** we can generate blobs of points with Gaussian distribution as follows:

```
from sklearn.datasets import make_blobs
X, y = make_blobs(300, 2, centers=2, random_state=2,
cluster_std=1.5)
plt.scatter(X[:, 0], X[:, 1], c=y, s=50,
cmap='summer');
```

Next, for using **GaussianNB** model, we need to import and make its object as follows:

```
from sklearn.naive_bayes import GaussianNB
model_GBN = GaussianNB()
model_GNB.fit(X, y);
```

Now, we have to do prediction. It can be done after generating some new data as follows:

```
rng = np.random.RandomState(0)
Xnew = [-6, -14] + [14, 18] * rng.rand(2000, 2)
ynew = model_GNB.predict(Xnew)
```

Next, we are plotting new data to find its boundaries:

```
plt.scatter(X[:, 0], X[:, 1], c=y, s=50,
cmap='summer')
lim = plt.axis()
plt.scatter(Xnew[:, 0], Xnew[:, 1], c=ynew, s=20,
cmap='summer', alpha=0.1)
plt.axis(lim);
```

Now, with the help of following line of codes, we can find the posterior probabilities of first and second label:

```
yprob = model_GNB.predict_proba(Xnew)
yprob[-10:].round(3)
```

Output

```
array([[0.998, 0.002],
       [1.   , 0.   ],
       [0.987, 0.013],
       [1.   , 0.   ],
       [1.   , 0.   ],
       [1.   , 0.   ],
       [1.   , 0.   ],
       [1.   , 0.   ],
       [0.   , 1.   ],
       [0.986, 0.014]])
```

Pros & Cons

Pros

The followings are some pros of using Naïve Bayes classifiers:

- Naïve Bayes classification is easy to implement and fast.
- It will converge faster than discriminative models like logistic regression.
- It requires less training data.
- It is highly scalable in nature, or they scale linearly with the number of predictors and data points.
- It can make probabilistic predictions and can handle

continuous as well as discrete data.
- Naïve Bayes classification algorithm can be used for binary as well as multi-class classification problems both.

Cons

The followings are some cons of using Naïve Bayes classifiers:

- One of the most important cons of Naïve Bayes classification is its strong feature independence because in real life it is almost impossible to have a set of features which are completely independent of each other.
- Another issue with Naïve Bayes classification is its 'zero frequency' which means that if a categorial variable has a category but not being observed in training data set, then Naïve Bayes model will assign a zero probability to it and it will be unable to make a prediction.

Applications of Naïve Bayes classification

The following are some common applications of Naïve Bayes classification:

Real-time prediction: Due to its ease of implementation and fast computation, it can be used to do prediction in real-time.

Multi-class prediction: Naïve Bayes classification algorithm can be used to predict posterior probability of multiple classes of target variable.

Text classification: Due to the feature of multi-class prediction, Naïve Bayes classification algorithms are well suited for text classification. That is why it is also used to solve problems like spam-filtering and sentiment analysis.

Recommendation system: Along with the algorithms like collaborative filtering, Naïve Bayes makes a Recommendation system which can be used to filter unseen information and to predict weather a user would like the given resource or not.

Random Forest

Random forest is a supervised learning algorithm which is used for both classification as well as regression. But however, it is mainly used for classification problems. As we know that a forest is made up of trees and more trees means more robust forest. Similarly, random forest algorithm creates decision trees on data samples and then gets the prediction from each of them and finally selects the best solution by means of voting. It is an ensemble method which is better than a single decision tree because it reduces the over-fitting by averaging the result.

Working of Random Forest Algorithm

We can understand the working of Random Forest algorithm with the help of following steps:

- **Step 1:** First, start with the selection of random samples from a given dataset.
- **Step 2:** Next, this algorithm will construct a decision tree for every sample. Then it will get the prediction result from every decision tree.
- **Step 3:** In this step, voting will be performed for every predicted result.

- **Step 4:** At last, select the most voted prediction result as the final prediction result.

The following diagram will illustrate its working:

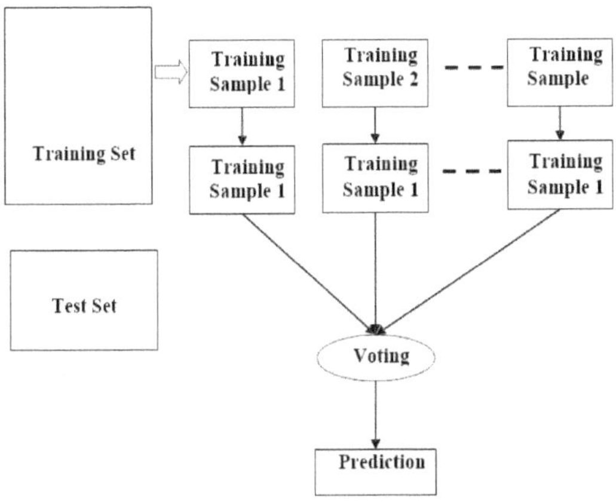

Implementation in Python

First, start with importing necessary Python packages:

```
import numpy as np
import matplotlib.pyplot as plt import pandas as pd
```

Next, download the iris dataset from its weblink as follows:

```
path =
"https://archive.ics.uci.edu/ml/machine-learning-
databases/iris/iris.data"
```

Next, we need to assign column names to the dataset as follows:

```
headernames = ['sepal-length','sepal-width',
'petal-length', 'petal-width',
'Class']
```

Now, we need to read dataset to **pandasdataframe** as follows:

```
dataset = pd.read_csv(path, names=headernames)
dataset.head()
```

	sepal-length	sepal-width	petal-length	petal-width	Class
0	5.1	3.5	1.4	0.2	Iris-setosa
1	4.9	3.0	1.4	0.2	Iris-setosa
2	4.7	3.2	1.3	0.2	Iris-setosa
3	4.6	3.1	1.5	0.2	Iris-setosa
4	5.0	3.6	1.4	0.2	Iris-setosa

Data Preprocessing will be done with the help of following script lines:

```
X = dataset.iloc[:, :-1].values y = dataset.iloc[:,
4].values
```

Next, we will divide the data into train and test split. The following code will split the dataset into 70% training data and 30% of testing data:

```
from sklearn.model_selectionimport train_test_split
X_train, X_test, y_train, y_test =
train_test_split(X, y, test_size=0.30)
```

Next, train the model with the help of **RandomForestClassifi er** class of **sklearn** as follows:

```
from sklearn.ensemble import RandomForestClassifier
classifier = RandomForestClassifier(n_estimators=50)
classifier.fit(X_train, y_train)
```

At last, we need to make prediction. It can be done with the help of following script:

```
y_pred = classifier.predict(X_test)
Next, print the results as follows:
from sklearn.metrics import classification_report,
confusion_matrix, accuracy_score
result = confusion_matrix(y_test, y_pred)
print("Confusion Matrix:")
print(result)
result1 = classification_report(y_test, y_pred)
print("Classification Report:",)
print (result1)
result2 = accuracy_score(y_test,y_pred)
print("Accuracy:",result2)
```

Output

```
Confusion Matrix:
[[14  0  0]
 [ 0 18  1]
 [ 0  0 12]]
Classification Report:
               precision    recall  f1-score   support

  Iris-setosa       1.00      1.00      1.00        14
Iris-versicolor     1.00      0.95      0.97        19
 Iris-virginica     0.92      1.00      0.96        12


    micro avg       0.98      0.98      0.98        45
    macro avg       0.97      0.98      0.98        45
 weighted avg       0.98      0.98      0.98        45


Accuracy: 0.9777777777777777
```

Pros and Cons of Random Forest

Pros

The following are the advantages of Random Forest algorithm:

- It overcomes the problem of over fitting by averaging or combining the results of different decision trees.
- Random forests work well for a large range of data items than a single decision tree does.
- Random forest has less variance then single decision tree.
- Random forests are very flexible and possess very high accuracy.
- Scaling of data does not require in random forest algorithm. It maintains good accuracy even after providing data without scaling.

- Random Forest algorithms maintains good accuracy even a large proportion of the data is missing.

Cons

The following are the disadvantages of Random Forest algorithm:

- Complexity is the main disadvantage of Random forest algorithms.
- Construction of Random forests are much harder and time-consuming than decision trees.
- More computational resources are required to implement Random Forest algorithm.
- It is less intuitive in case when we have a large collection of decision trees.
- The prediction process using random forests is very time-consuming in comparison with other algorithms.

Regression

Regression is another important and broadly used statistical and machine learning tool. The key objective of regression-based tasks is to predict output labels or responses which are continued numeric values, for the given input data. The output will be based on what the model has learned in training phase. Basically, regression models use the input data features (independent variables) and their corresponding continuous numeric output values (dependent or outcome variables) to learn specific association between inputs and corresponding outputs.

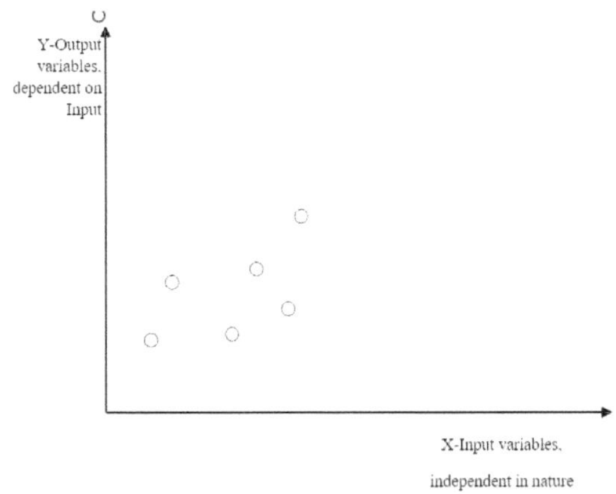

Types of Regression Models

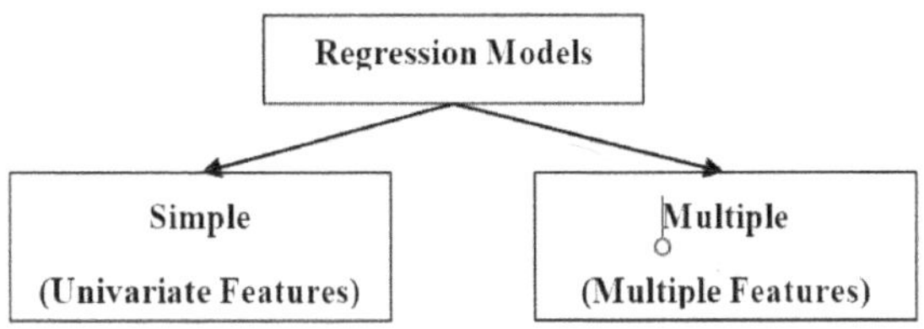

Regression models are of following two types:

Simple regression model: This is the most basic regression model in which predictions are formed from a single, univariate feature of the data.

Multiple regression model: As name implies, in this regression model the predictions are formed from multiple features of the data.

Building a Regressorin Python

Regressor model in Python can be constructed just like we constructed the classifier. Scikit-learn, a Python library for machine learning can also be used to build a regressor in Python.

In the following example, we will be building basic regression model that will fit a line to the data i.e. linear regressor. The necessary steps for building a regressor in Python are as follows:

Step 1: Importing necessary python package

For building a regressor using scikit-learn, we need to import it along with other necessary packages. We can import the by using following script:

```
import numpy as np
from sklearn import linear_model import
sklearn.metrics as sm
import matplotlib.pyplot as plt
```

Step 2: Importing dataset

After importing necessary package, we need a dataset to build regression prediction model. We can import it from sklearn dataset or can use other one as per our requirement. We are going to use our saved input data. We can import it with the help of following script:

```
input = r'C:\linear.txt'
```

Next, we need to load this data. We are using **np.loadtxt** function to load it.

```
input_data = np.loadtxt(input,delimiter=',')
X, y = input_data[:, :-1], input_data[:, -1]
```

Step 3: Organizing data into training & testing sets

As we need to test our model on unseen data hence, we will divide our dataset into two parts: a training set and a test set. The following command will perform it:

```
training_samples = int(0.6 * len(X))
testing_samples = len(X) - num_training
X_train, y_train = X[:training_samples],
y[:training_samples] X_test, y_test =
X[training_samples:], y[training_samples:]
```

Step 4- Model evaluation & prediction

After dividing the data into training and testing we need to build the model. We will be using **LineaRegression()** function of Scikit-learn for this purpose. Following command will create a linear regressor object.

```
reg_linear= linear_model.LinearRegression()
```

Next, train this model with the training samples as follows:

```
reg_linear.fit(X_train, y_train)
```

Now, at last we need to do the prediction with the testing data.

```
y_test_pred = reg_linear.predict(X_test)
```

Step 5 –Plot & visualization

After prediction, we can plot and visualize it with the help of
following script:

```
plt.scatter(X_test, y_test, color='red')
plt.plot(X_test, y_test_pred, color='black',
linewidth=2)
plt.xticks(()) plt.yticks(()) plt.show()
```

Output

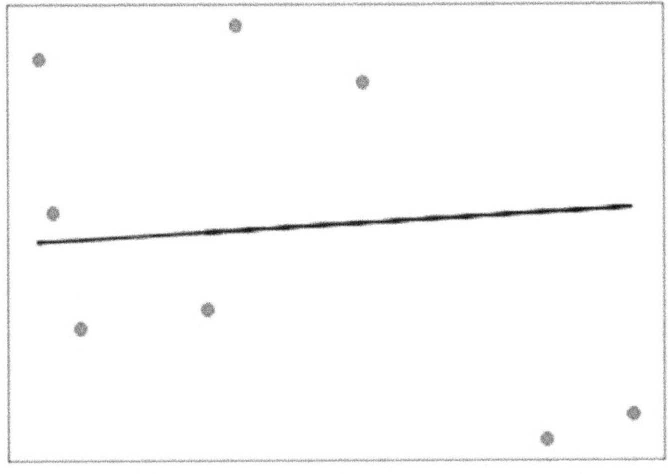

In the above output, we can see the regression line between the data points.

Step 6– Performance computation: We can also compute the performance of our regression model with the help of various performance metrics as follows:

```
print("Regressor model performance:")
print("Mean absolute error(MAE)
=",round(sm.mean_absolute_error(y_test,
y_test_pred), 2))
print("Mean squared error(MSE) =",
round(sm.mean_squared_error(y_test, y_test_pred), 2))
print("Median absolute error =",
round(sm.median_absolute_error(y_test, y_test_pred),
2))
print("Explain variance score
=",round(sm.explained_variance_score(y_test,
```

```
y_test_pred), 2))
print("R2 score =",round(sm.r2_score(y_test,
y_test_pred), 2))
```

Output

```
Regressor model performance: Meanabsolute error(MAE)
= 1.78
Mean squared error(MSE) = 3.89
Median absolute error = 2.01
Explain variance score = -0.09
R2 score = -0.09
```

Types of ML Regression Algorithms

The most useful and popular ML regression algorithm is Linear regression algorithm which further divided into two types namely:

- Simple Linear Regression algorithm.
- Multiple Linear Regression algorithm.

We will discuss about it and implement it in Python in the next chapter.

Applications

The applications of ML regression algorithms are as follows:

Forecasting or Predictive analysis: One of the important uses of regression is forecasting or predictive analysis. For example, we can forecast GDP, oil prices or in simple words the quantitative data that changes with the passage of time.

Optimization: We can optimize business processes with the help of regression. For example, a store manager can create a statistical model to understand the peek time of coming of customers.

Error correction: In business, taking correct decision is equally important as optimizing the business process. Regression can help us to take correct decision as well in correcting the already implemented decision.

Economics: It is the most used tool in economics. We can use regression to predict supply, demand, consumption, inventory investment etc.

Finance: A financial company is always interested in minimizing the risk portfolio and want to know the factors that affects the customers. All these can be predicted with the help of regression model.

Linear Regression

Linear regression is probably one of the most important and widely used regression techniques. It's among the simplest regression methods. One of its main advantages is the ease of interpreting results.

Problem Formulation

When implementing linear regression of some dependent variable y on the set of independent variables $\mathbf{x} = (x_1, ..., x_r)$, where r is the number of predictors, you assume a linear relationship between y and $\mathbf{x}$: $y = \beta_0 + \beta_1 x_1 + \cdots + \beta_r x_r + \varepsilon$. This equation is the regression equation. $\beta_0, \beta_1, ..., \beta_r$ are the regression coefficients, and ε is the random error.

Linear regression calculates the estimators of the regression coefficients or simply the predicted weights, denoted with b_0, $b_1, ..., b_r$. These estimators define the estimated regression function $f(\mathbf{x}) = b_0 + b_1 x_1 + \cdots + b_r x_r$. This function should capture the dependencies between the inputs and output sufficiently well.

The estimated or predicted response, $f(\mathbf{x}_i)$, for each observation $i = 1, ..., n$, should be as close as possible to the corresponding actual response y_i. The differences $y_i - f(\mathbf{x}_i)$ for all observations $i = 1, ..., n$, are called the residuals. Regression is about determining the best predicted weights—that is, the weights corresponding to the smallest residuals.

To get the best weights, you usually minimize the sum of squared residuals (SSR) for all observations $i = 1, ..., n$: SSR = $\Sigma_i(y_i - f(\mathbf{x}_i))^2$. This approach is called the method of ordinary least squares.

Regression Performance

The variation of actual responses y_i, $i = 1, ..., n$, occurs partly due to the dependence on the predictors $\mathbf{x}_i$. However, there's also an additional inherent variance of the output.

The coefficient of determination, denoted as R^2, tells you which amount of variation in y can be explained by the dependence on $\mathbf{x}$, using the particular regression model. A larger R^2 indicates a better fit and means that the model can better explain the variation of the output with different inputs.

The value $R^2 = 1$ corresponds to SSR = 0. That's the perfect fit, since the values of predicted and actual responses fit completely to each other.

Simple Linear Regression

Simple or single-variate linear regression is the simplest case of linear regression, as it has a single independent variable, x

$= x.$

The following figure illustrates simple linear regression:

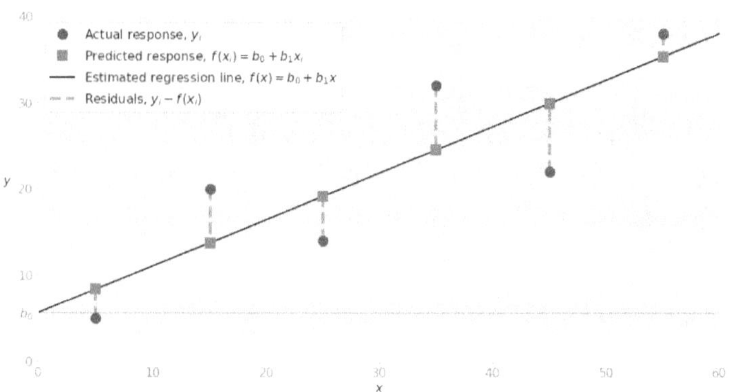

Example of simple linear regression

When implementing simple linear regression, you typically start with a given set of input-output (x-y) pairs. These pairs are your observations, shown as green circles in the figure. For example, the leftmost observation has the input $x = 5$ and the actual output, or response, $y = 5$. The next one has $x = 15$ and $y = 20$, and so on.

The estimated regression function, represented by the black line, has the equation $f(x) = b_0 + b_1 x$. Your goal is to calculate the optimal values of the predicted weights b_0 and b_1 that minimize SSR and determine the estimated regression function.

The value of b_0, also called the intercept, shows the point where the estimated regression line crosses the y axis. It's the value of the estimated response $f(x)$ for $x = 0$. The value of b_1 determines the slope of the estimated regression line.

The predicted responses, shown as red squares, are the points on the regression line that correspond to the input values. For example, for the input $x = 5$, the predicted response is $f(5) = 8.33$, which the leftmost red square represents.

The vertical dashed grey lines represent the residuals, which can be calculated as $y_i - f(\mathbf{x}_i) = y_i - b_0 - b_1 x_i$ for $i = 1, \ldots, n$. They're the distances between the green circles and red squares. When you implement linear regression, you're actually trying to minimize these distances and make the red squares as close to the predefined green circles as possible.

Multiple Linear Regression

Multiple or multivariate linear regression is a case of linear regression with two or more independent variables.

If there are just two independent variables, then the estimated regression function is $f(x_1, x_2) = b_0 + b_1 x_1 + b_2 x_2$. It represents a regression plane in a three-dimensional space. The goal of regression is to determine the values of the weights b_0, b_1, and b_2 such that this plane is as close as possible to the actual responses, while yielding the minimal SSR.

The case of more than two independent variables is similar, but more general. The estimated regression function is $f(x_1, \ldots, x_r) = b_0 + b_1 x_1 + \cdots + b_r x_r$, and there are $r + 1$ weights to be determined when the number of inputs is r.

Polynomial Regression

You can regard polynomial regression as a generalized case of linear regression. You assume the polynomial dependence between the output and inputs and, consequently, the polynomial estimated regression function.

In other words, in addition to linear terms like $b_1 x_1$, your regression function f can include nonlinear terms such as $b_2 x_1{}^2$, $b_3 x_1{}^3$, or even $b_4 x_1 x_2$, $b_5 x_1{}^2 x_2$.

The simplest example of polynomial regression has a single independent variable, and the estimated regression function is a polynomial of degree two: $f(x) = b_0 + b_1 x + b_2 x^2$.

Now, remember that you want to calculate b_0, b_1, and b_2 to minimize SSR. These are your unknowns!

Keeping this in mind, compare the previous regression function with the function $f(x_1, x_2) = b_0 + b_1 x_1 + b_2 x_2$, used for linear regression. They look very similar and are both linear functions of the unknowns b_0, b_1, and b_2. This is why you can solve the polynomial regression problem as a linear problem with the term x^2 regarded as an input variable.

In the case of two variables and the polynomial of degree two, the regression function has this form: $f(x_1, x_2) = b_0 + b_1 x_1 + b_2 x_2 + b_3 x_1{}^2 + b_4 x_1 x_2 + b_5 x_2{}^2$.

The procedure for solving the problem is identical to the previous case. You apply linear regression for five inputs: x_1,

x_2, $x_1{}^2$, $x_1 x_2$, and $x_2{}^2$. As the result of regression, you get the values of six weights that minimize SSR: b_0, b_1, b_2, b_3, b_4, and b_5.

Of course, there are more general problems, but this should be enough to illustrate the point.

Underfitting and Overfitting

One very important question that might arise when you're implementing polynomial regression is related to the choice of the optimal degree of the polynomial regression function.

There's no straightforward rule for doing this. It depends on the case. You should, however, be aware of two problems that might follow the choice of the degree: underfitting and overfitting.

Underfitting occurs when a model can't accurately capture the dependencies among data, usually as a consequence of its own simplicity. It often yields a low R^2 with known data and bad generalization capabilities when applied with new data.

Overfitting happens when a model learns both data dependencies and random fluctuations. In other words, a model learns the existing data too well. Complex models, which have many features or terms, are often prone to overfitting. When applied to known data, such models usually yield high R^2. However, they often don't generalize well and have significantly lower R^2 when used with new data.

The next figure illustrates the underfitted, well-fitted, and overfitted models:

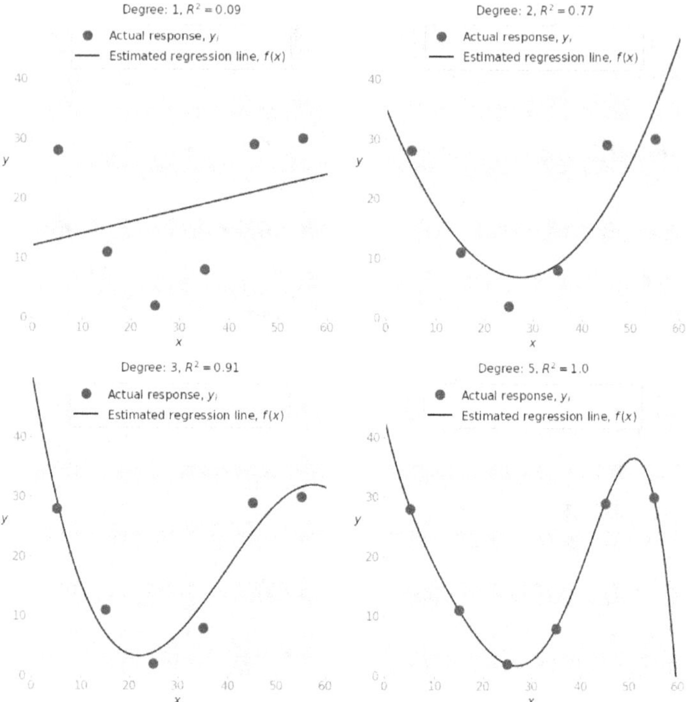

Example of underfitted, well-fitted and overfitted models

The top-left plot shows a linear regression line that has a low R^2. It might also be important that a straight line can't take into account the fact that the actual response increases as x moves away from twenty-five and toward zero. This is likely an example of underfitting.

The top-right plot illustrates polynomial regression with the degree equal to two. In this instance, this might be the optimal degree for modeling this data. The model has a value of R^2 that's satisfactory in many cases and shows trends nicely.

The bottom-left plot presents polynomial regression with the degree equal to three. The value of R^2 is higher than in the preceding cases. This model behaves better with known data than the previous ones. However, it shows some signs of overfitting, especially for the input values close to sixy, where the line starts decreasing, although the actual data doesn't show that.

Finally, on the bottom-right plot, you can see the perfect fit: six points and the polynomial line of the degree five (or higher) yield $R^2 = 1$. Each actual response equals its corresponding prediction.

In some situations, this might be exactly what you're looking for. In many cases, however, this is an overfitted model. It's likely to have poor behavior with unseen data, especially with the inputs larger than fifty.

For example, it assumes, without any evidence, that there's a significant drop in responses for x greater than fifty and that y reaches zero for x near sixty. Such behavior is the consequence of excessive effort to learn and fit the existing data.

Python Packages for Linear Regression

It's time to start implementing linear regression in Python. To do this, you'll apply the proper packages and their functions and classes.

NumPy is a fundamental Python scientific package that allows many high-performance operations on single-dimensional and multidimensional arrays. It also offers many mathematical routines. Of course, it's open-source.

The package scikit-learn is a widely used Python library for machine learning, built on top of NumPy and some other packages. It provides the means for preprocessing data, reducing dimensionality, implementing regression, classifying, clustering, and more. Like NumPy, scikit-learn is also open-source.

If you want to implement linear regression and need functionality beyond the scope of scikit-learn, you should consider stats models. It's a powerful Python package for the estimation of statistical models, performing tests, and more. It's open-source as well.

Simple Linear Regression With scikit-learn

You'll start with the simplest case, which is simple linear regression. There are five basic steps when you're implementing linear regression:

1. Import the packages and classes that you need.

2. Provide data to work with, and eventually do appropriate transformations.
3. Create a regression model and fit it with existing data.
4. Check the results of model fitting to know whether the model is satisfactory.
5. Apply the model for predictions.

These steps are more or less general for most of the regression approaches and implementations. Throughout the rest of the tutorial, you'll learn how to do these steps for several different scenarios.

Step 1: Import packages and classes

The first step is to import the package numpy and the class LinearRegression from sklearn.linear_model:

```
>>> import numpy as np
>>> from sklearn.linear_model import LinearRegression
```

Now, you have all the functionalities that you need to implement linear regression.

The fundamental data type of NumPy is the array type called numpy.ndarray. The rest of this tutorial uses the term array to refer to instances of the type numpy.ndarray.

You'll use the class sklearn.linear_model.LinearRegression to perform linear and polynomial regression and make predictions accordingly.

Step 2: Provide data

The second step is defining data to work with. The inputs (regressors, x) and output (response, y) should be arrays or similar objects. This is the simplest way of providing data for regression:

```
>>> x = np.array([5, 15, 25, 35, 45,
55]).reshape((-1, 1))
>>> y = np.array([5, 20, 14, 32, 22, 38])
```

Now, you have two arrays: the input, x, and the output, y. You should call .reshape() on x because this array must be two-dimensional, or more precisely, it must have one column and as many rows as necessary. That's exactly what the argument (-1, 1) of .reshape() specifies.

This is how x and y look now:

```
>>> x
array([[ 5],
       [15],
       [25],
       [35],
       [45],
       [55]])
>>> y
array([ 5, 20, 14, 32, 22, 38])
```

As you can see, x has two dimensions, and x.shape is (6, 1), while y has a single dimension, and y.shape is (6,).

Step 3: Create a model and fit it

The next step is to create a linear regression model and fit it using the existing data. Create an instance of the class LinearRegression, which will represent the regression model:

```
>>> model = LinearRegression()
```

This statement creates the variable model as an instance of LinearRegression. You can provide several optional parameters to LinearRegression:

- fit_intercept is a Boolean that, if True, decides to calculate the intercept b_0 or, if False, considers it equal to zero. It defaults to True.
- normalize is a Boolean that, if True, decides to normalize the input variables. It defaults to False, in which case it doesn't normalize the input variables.
- copy_X is a Boolean that decides whether to copy (True) or overwrite the input variables (False). It's True by default.
- n_jobs is either an integer or None. It represents the number of jobs used in parallel computation. It defaults to None, which usually means one job. -1 means to use all available processors.

Your model as defined above uses the default values of all parameters. It's time to start using the model. First, you need to call .fit() on model:

```
>>> model.fit(x, y)
LinearRegression()
```

With .fit(), you calculate the optimal values of the weights b_0 and b_1, using the existing input and output, x and y, as the arguments. In other words, .fit() fits the model. It returns self, which is the variable model itself. That's why you can replace the last two statements with this one:

```
>>> model = LinearRegression().fit(x, y)
```

This statement does the same thing as the previous two. It's just shorter.

Step 4: Get results

Once you have your model fitted, you can get the results to check whether the model works satisfactorily and to interpret it. You can obtain the coefficient of determination, R^2, with .score() called on model:

```
>>> r_sq = model.score(x, y)
>>> print(f"coefficient of determination: {r_sq}")
coefficient of determination: 0.7158756137479542
```

When you're applying .score(), the arguments are also the predictor x and response y, and the return value is R^2.

The attributes of model are .intercept_, which represents the coefficient b_0, and .coef_, which represents b_1:

```
>>> print(f"intercept: {model.intercept_}")
intercept: 5.633333333333329

>>> print(f"slope: {model.coef_}")
slope: [0.54]
```

The code above illustrates how to get b_0 and b_1. You can notice that .intercept_ is a scalar, while .coef_ is an array.

Note: In scikit-learn, by convention, a trailing underscore indicates that an attribute is estimated. In this example, .intercept_ and .coef_ are estimated values.

The value of b_0 is approximately 5.63. This illustrates that your model predicts the response 5.63 when x is zero. The value b_1 = 0.54 means that the predicted response rises by 0.54 when x is increased by one.

You'll notice that you can provide y as a two-dimensional array as well. In this case, you'll get a similar result. This is how it might look:

```
>>> new_model = LinearRegression().fit(x,
y.reshape((-1, 1)))
>>> print(f"intercept: {new_model.intercept_}")
intercept: [5.63333333]
>>> print(f"slope: {new_model.coef_}")
slope: [[0.54]]
```

As you can see, this example is very similar to the previous one, but in this case, .intercept_ is a one-dimensional array with the single element b_0, and .coef_ is a two-dimensional array with the single element b_1.

Step 5: Predict response

Once you have a satisfactory model, then you can use it for predictions with either existing or new data. To obtain the predicted response, use .predict():

```
>>> y_pred = model.predict(x)
>>> print(f"predicted response:\n{y_pred}")
predicted response:
[ 8.33333333 13.73333333 19.13333333 24.53333333
29.93333333 35.33333333]
```

When applying .predict(), you pass the regressor as the argument and get the corresponding predicted response. This is a nearly identical way to predict the response:

```
>>> y_pred = model.intercept_ + model.coef_ * x
>>> print(f"predicted response:\n{y_pred}")
predicted response:
[[ 8.33333333]
 [13.73333333]
 [19.13333333]
 [24.53333333]
 [29.93333333]
 [35.33333333]]
```

In this case, you multiply each element of x with model.coef_ and add model.intercept_ to the product.

The output here differs from the previous example only in dimensions. The predicted response is now a two-dimensional array, while in the previous case, it had one dimension.

If you reduce the number of dimensions of x to one, then these two approaches will yield the same result. You can do this by replacing x with x.reshape(-1), x.flatten(), or x.ravel() when multiplying it with model.coef_.

In practice, regression models are often applied for forecasts. This means that you can use fitted models to calculate the outputs based on new inputs:

```
>>> x_new = np.arange(5).reshape((-1, 1))
>>> x_new
array([[0],
       [1],
       [2],
       [3],
       [4]])
>>> y_new = model.predict(x_new)
>>> y_new
array([5.63333333, 6.17333333, 6.71333333,
7.25333333, 7.79333333])
```

Here .predict() is applied to the new regressor x_new and yields the response y_new. This example conveniently uses arange() from numpy to generate an array with the elements from 0, inclusive, up to but excluding 5—that is, 0, 1, 2, 3, and 4.

Multiple Linear Regression With scikit-learn

You can implement multiple linear regression following the same steps as you would for simple regression. The main difference is that your x array will now have two or more columns.

Steps 1 and 2: Import packages and classes, and provide data

First, you import numpy and sklearn.linear_model.Linear-Regression and provide known inputs and output:

```
>>> import numpy as np
>>> from sklearn.linear_model import LinearRegression

>>> x = [
...    [0, 1], [5, 1], [15, 2], [25, 5], [35, 11],
[45, 15], [55, 34], [60, 35]
... ]
>>> y = [4, 5, 20, 14, 32, 22, 38, 43]
>>> x, y = np.array(x), np.array(y)
```

That's a simple way to define the input x and output y. You can print x and y to see how they look now:

```
>>> x
array([[ 0,  1],
       [ 5,  1],
       [15,  2],
       [25,  5],
       [35, 11],
       [45, 15],
       [55, 34],
       [60, 35]])
```

```
>>> y
array([ 4,   5, 20, 14, 32, 22, 38, 43])
```

In multiple linear regression, x is a two-dimensional array with at least two columns, while y is usually a one-dimensional array. This is a simple example of multiple linear regression, and x has exactly two columns.

Step 3: Create a model and fit it

The next step is to create the regression model as an instance of LinearRegression and fit it with .fit():

```
>>> model = LinearRegression().fit(x, y)
```

The result of this statement is the variable model referring to the object of type LinearRegression. It represents the regression model fitted with existing data.

Step 4: Get results

You can obtain the properties of the model the same way as in the case of simple linear regression:

```
>>> r_sq = model.score(x, y)
>>> print(f"coefficient of determination: {r_sq}")
coefficient of determination: 0.8615939258756776

>>> print(f"intercept: {model.intercept_}")
intercept: 5.52257927519819
```

```
>>> print(f"coefficients: {model.coef_}")
coefficients: [0.44706965 0.25502548]
```

You obtain the value of R^2 using .score() and the values of the estimators of regression coefficients with .intercept_ and .coef_. Again, .intercept_ holds the bias b_0, while now .coef_ is an array containing b_1 and b_2.

In this example, the intercept is approximately 5.52, and this is the value of the predicted response when $x_1 = x_2 = 0$. An increase of x_1 by 1 yields a rise of the predicted response by 0.45. Similarly, when x_2 grows by 1, the response rises by 0.26.

Step 5: Predict response

Predictions also work the same way as in the case of simple linear regression:

```
>>> y_pred = model.predict(x)
>>> print(f"predicted response:\n{y_pred}")
predicted response:
[ 5.77760476  8.012953    12.73867497 17.9744479
23.97529728 29.4660957
 38.78227633 41.27265006]
```

The predicted response is obtained with .predict(), which is equivalent to the following:

```
>>> y_pred = model.intercept_ + np.sum(model.coef_ *
x, axis=1)
>>> print(f"predicted response:\n{y_pred}")
predicted response:
```

```
[  5.77760476  8.012953     12.73867497 17.9744479
23.97529728 29.4660957
 38.78227633 41.27265006]
```

You can predict the output values by multiplying each column of the input with the appropriate weight, summing the results, and adding the intercept to the sum.

You can apply this model to new data as well:

```
>>> x_new = np.arange(10).reshape((-1, 2))
>>> x_new
array([[0, 1],
       [2, 3],
       [4, 5],
       [6, 7],
       [8, 9]])
>>> y_new = model.predict(x_new)
>>> y_new
array([ 5.77760476,  7.18179502,  8.58598528,
9.99017554, 11.3943658 ])
```

That's the prediction using a linear regression model.

Polynomial Regression With scikit-learn

Implementing polynomial regression with scikit-learn is very similar to linear regression. There's only one extra step: you need to transform the array of inputs to include nonlinear terms such as x^2.

Step 1: Import packages and classes

In addition to numpy and sklearn.linear_model.LinearRegression, you should also import the class PolynomialFeatures from sklearn.preprocessing:

```
>>> import numpy as np
>>> from sklearn.linear_model import LinearRegression
>>> from sklearn.preprocessing import
PolynomialFeatures
```

The import is now done, and you have everything you need to work with.

Step 2a: Provide data

This step defines the input and output and is the same as in the case of linear regression:

```
>>> x = np.array([5, 15, 25, 35, 45,
55]).reshape((-1, 1))
>>> y = np.array([15, 11, 2, 8, 25, 32])
```

Now you have the input and output in a suitable format. Keep in mind that you need the input to be a two-dimensional array. That's why .reshape() is used.

Step 2b: Transform input data

This is the new step that you need to implement for polynomial regression! As you learned earlier, you need to include x^2—and perhaps other terms—as additional features when implementing polynomial regression. For that reason, you should transform the input array x to contain any additional columns with the values of x^2, and eventually more features.

It's possible to transform the input array in several ways, like using insert() from numpy. But the class PolynomialFeatures is very convenient for this purpose. Go ahead and create an instance of this class:

```
>>> transformer = PolynomialFeatures(degree=2,
 include_bias=False)
```

The variable transformer refers to an instance of PolynomialFeatures that you can use to transform the input x.

You can provide several optional parameters to PolynomialFeatures:

- degree is an integer (2 by default) that represents the degree of the polynomial regression function.
- interaction_only is a Boolean (False by default) that decides whether to include only interaction features (True) or all features (False).
- include_bias is a Boolean (True by default) that decides whether to include the bias, or intercept, column of 1 values (True) or not (False).

This example uses the default values of all parameters except include_bias. You'll sometimes want to experiment with the degree of the function, and it can be beneficial for readability to provide this argument anyway.

Before applying transformer, you need to fit it with .fit():

```
>>> transformer.fit(x)
PolynomialFeatures(include_bias=False)
```

Once transformer is fitted, then it's ready to create a new, modified input array. You apply .transform() to do that:

```
>>> x_ = transformer.transform(x)
```

That's the transformation of the input array with .transform(). It takes the input array as the argument and returns the modified array.

You can also use .fit_transform() to replace the three previous statements with only one:

```
>>> x_ = PolynomialFeatures(degree=2,
include_bias=False).fit_transform(x)
```

With .fit_transform(), you're fitting and transforming the input array in one statement. This method also takes the input array and effectively does the same thing as .fit() and .transform() called in that order. It also returns the modified array. This is how the new input array looks:

```
>>> x_
array([[    5.,    25.],
       [   15.,   225.],
       [   25.,   625.],
       [   35.,  1225.],
```

```
      [  45., 2025.],
      [  55., 3025.]])
```

The modified input array contains two columns: one with the original inputs and the other with their squares.

Step 3: Create a model and fit it

This step is also the same as in the case of linear regression. You create and fit the model:

```
>>> model = LinearRegression().fit(x_, y)
```

The regression model is now created and fitted. It's ready for application. You should keep in mind that the first argument of .fit() is the *modified input array* x_ and not the original x.

Step 4: Get results

You can obtain the properties of the model the same way as in the case of linear regression:

```
>>> r_sq = model.score(x_, y)
>>> print(f"coefficient of determination: {r_sq}")
coefficient of determination: 0.8908516262498563

>>> print(f"intercept: {model.intercept_}")
intercept: 21.372321428571436

>>> print(f"coefficients: {model.coef_}")
coefficients: [-1.32357143  0.02839286]
```

Again, .score() returns R^2. Its first argument is also the modified input x_, not x. The values of the weights are associated to .intercept_ and .coef_. Here, .intercept_ represents b_0, while .coef_ references the array that contains b_1 and b_2.

You can obtain a very similar result with different transformation and regression arguments:

```
>>> x_ = PolynomialFeatures(degree=2,
include_bias=True).fit_transform(x)
```

If you call PolynomialFeatures with the default parameter include_bias=True, or if you just omit it, then you'll obtain the new input array x_ with the additional leftmost column containing only 1 values. This column corresponds to the intercept. This is how the modified input array looks in this case:

```
>>> x_
array([[1.000e+00, 5.000e+00, 2.500e+01],
       [1.000e+00, 1.500e+01, 2.250e+02],
       [1.000e+00, 2.500e+01, 6.250e+02],
       [1.000e+00, 3.500e+01, 1.225e+03],
       [1.000e+00, 4.500e+01, 2.025e+03],
       [1.000e+00, 5.500e+01, 3.025e+03]])
```

The first column of x_ contains ones, the second has the values of x, while the third holds the squares of x.

The intercept is already included with the leftmost column of ones, and you don't need to include it again when creating the instance of LinearRegression. Thus, you can provide fit_intercept=False. This is how the next statement looks:

```
>>> model =
LinearRegression(fit_intercept=False).fit(x_, y)
```

The variable model again corresponds to the new input array x_. Therefore, x_ should be passed as the first argument instead of x.

This approach yields the following results, which are similar to the previous case:

```
>>> r_sq = model.score(x_, y)
>>> print(f"coefficient of determination: {r_sq}")
coefficient of determination: 0.89085162262498564

>>> print(f"intercept: {model.intercept_}")
intercept: 0.0

>>> print(f"coefficients: {model.coef_}")
coefficients: [21.37232143 -1.32357143  0.02839286]
```

You see that now .intercept_ is zero, but .coef_ actually contains b_0 as its first element. Everything else is the same.

Step 5: Predict response

If you want to get the predicted response, just use .predict(), but remember that the argument should be the modified input x_ instead of the old x:

```
>>> y_pred = model.predict(x_)
>>> print(f"predicted response:\n{y_pred}")
predicted response:
[15.46428571  7.90714286  6.02857143  9.82857143
19.30714286 34.46428571]
```

As you can see, the prediction works almost the same way as in the case of linear regression. It just requires the modified input instead of the original.

You can apply an identical procedure if you have several input variables. You'll have an input array with more than one column, but everything else will be the same. Here's an example:

```
>>> # Step 1: Import packages and classes
>>> import numpy as np
>>> from sklearn.linear_model import LinearRegression
>>> from sklearn.preprocessing import
PolynomialFeatures

>>> # Step 2a: Provide data
>>> x = [
...     [0, 1], [5, 1], [15, 2], [25, 5], [35, 11],
[45, 15], [55, 34], [60, 35]
... ]
>>> y = [4, 5, 20, 14, 32, 22, 38, 43]
>>> x, y = np.array(x), np.array(y)

>>> # Step 2b: Transform input data
>>> x_ = PolynomialFeatures(degree=2,
include_bias=False).fit_transform(x)

>>> # Step 3: Create a model and fit it
```

```
>>> model = LinearRegression().fit(x_, y)

>>> # Step 4: Get results
>>> r_sq = model.score(x_, y)
>>> intercept, coefficients = model.intercept_,
model.coef_

>>> # Step 5: Predict response
>>> y_pred = model.predict(x_)
```

This regression example yields the following results and predictions:

```
>>> print(f"coefficient of determination: {r_sq}")
coefficient of determination: 0.9453701449127822

>>> print(f"intercept: {intercept}")
intercept: 0.8430556452395876

>>> print(f"coefficients:\n{coefficients}")
coefficients:
[ 2.44828275  0.16160353 -0.15259677  0.47928683
-0.4641851 ]

>>> print(f"predicted response:\n{y_pred}")
predicted response:
[ 0.54047408 11.36340283 16.07809622 15.79139
29.73858619 23.50834636
 39.05631386 41.92339046]
```

In this case, there are six regression coefficients, including the intercept, as shown in the estimated regression function $f(x_1, x_2) = b_0 + b_1 x_1 + b_2 x_2 + b_3 x_1^2 + b_4 x_1 x_2 + b_5 x_2^2$.

You can also notice that polynomial regression yielded a higher coefficient of determination than multiple linear regression for the same problem. At first, you could think that obtaining such a large R^2 is an excellent result. It might be.

Advanced Linear Regression With statsmodels

You can implement linear regression in Python by using the package statsmodels as well. Typically, this is desirable when you need more detailed results.

The procedure is similar to that of scikit-learn.

Step 1: Import packages

First you need to do some imports. In addition to numpy, you need to import statsmodels.api:

```
>>> import numpy as np
>>> import statsmodels.api as sm
```

Now you have the packages that you need.

Step 2: Provide data and transform inputs

You can provide the inputs and outputs the same way as you did when you were using scikit-learn:

```
>>> x = [
...    [0, 1], [5, 1], [15, 2], [25, 5], [35, 11],
[45, 15], [55, 34], [60, 35]
... ]
>>> y = [4, 5, 20, 14, 32, 22, 38, 43]
>>> x, y = np.array(x), np.array(y)
```

The input and output arrays are created, but the job isn't done yet.

You need to add the column of ones to the inputs if you want statsmodels to calculate the intercept b_0. It doesn't take b_0 into account by default. This is just one function call:

```
>>> x = sm.add_constant(x)
```

That's how you add the column of ones to x with add_constant(). It takes the input array x as an argument and returns a new array with the column of ones inserted at the beginning. This is how x and y look now:

```
>>> x
array([[ 1.,   0.,   1.],
       [ 1.,   5.,   1.],
       [ 1., 15.,   2.],
       [ 1., 25.,   5.],
       [ 1., 35.,  11.],
       [ 1., 45.,  15.],
       [ 1., 55.,  34.],
       [ 1., 60.,  35.]])

>>> y
array([ 4,   5, 20, 14, 32, 22, 38, 43])
```

You can see that the modified x has three columns: the first column of ones, corresponding to b_0 and replacing the intercept, as well as two columns of the original features.

Step 3: Create a model and fit it

The regression model based on ordinary least squares is an instance of the class statsmodels.regression.linear_model.OLS. This is how you can obtain one:

```
>>> model = sm.OLS(y, x)
```

You should be careful here! Notice that the first argument is the output, followed by the input. This is the opposite order of the corresponding scikit-learn functions.

Once your model is created, then you can apply .fit() on it:

```
>>> results = model.fit()
```

By calling .fit(), you obtain the variable results, which is an instance of the class statsmodels.regression.linear_model.RegressionResultsWrapper. This object holds a lot of information about the regression model.

Step 4: Get results

The variable results refers to the object that contains detailed information about the results of linear regression. Explaining these results is far beyond the scope of this tutorial, but you'll learn here how to extract them.

You can call .summary() to get the table with the results of linear regression:

```
>>> print(results.summary())
OLS Regression Results
==============================================================================
Dep. Variable:                      y   R-squared:
                      0.862
Model:                            OLS   Adj.
R-squared:                      0.806
Method:                 Least Squares   F-statistic:
                      15.56
Date:                Thu, 12 May 2022   Prob
(F-statistic):                0.00713
Time:                        14:15:07
Log-Likelihood:                -24.316
No. Observations:                   8   AIC:
                      54.63
Df Residuals:                       5   BIC:
                      54.87
Df Model:                           2
Covariance Type:            nonrobust
==============================================================================
                 coef    std err          t
                P>|t|      [0.025      0.975]
------------------------------------------------------------------------------
const          5.5226      4.431      1.246
0.268         -5.867     16.912
x1             0.4471      0.285      1.567
0.178         -0.286      1.180
x2             0.2550      0.453      0.563
0.598         -0.910      1.420
==============================================================================
Omnibus:                        0.561
```

```
Durbin-Watson:                          3.268
Prob(Omnibus):                  0.755   Jarque-Bera
(JB):                   0.534
Skew:                           0.380   Prob(JB):
                        0.766
Kurtosis:                       1.987   Cond. No.
                        80.1
===========================================================

Warnings:
[1] Standard Errors assume that the covariance
matrix of the errors is correctly specified.
```

This table is very comprehensive. You can find many statistical values associated with linear regression, including R^2, b_0, b_1, and b_2.

In this particular case, you might obtain a warning saying kurtosistest only valid for n>=20. This is due to the small number of observations provided in the example.

You can extract any of the values from the table above. Here's an example:

```
>>> print(f"coefficient of determination:
{results.rsquared}")
coefficient of determination: 0.8615939258756776

>>> print(f"adjusted coefficient of determination:
{results.rsquared_adj}")
adjusted coefficient of determination:
0.8062314962259487

>>> print(f"regression coefficients:
```

```
{results.params}")
regression coefficients: [5.52257928 0.44706965
0.25502548]
```

That's how you obtain some of the results of linear regression:

1. .rsquared holds R^2.
2. .rsquared_adj represents adjusted R^2—that is, R^2 cor-
   rected according to the number of input features.
3. .params refers the array with b_0, b_1, and b_2.

You can also notice that these results are identical to those obtained with scikit-learn for the same problem.

Step 5: Predict response

You can obtain the predicted response on the input values used for creating the model using .fittedvalues or .predict() with the input array as the argument:

```
>>> print(f"predicted
response:\n{results.fittedvalues}")
predicted response:
[ 5.77760476  8.012953    12.73867497 17.9744479
23.97529728 29.4660957
 38.78227633 41.27265006]

>>> print(f"predicted
response:\n{results.predict(x)}")
predicted response:
[ 5.77760476  8.012953    12.73867497 17.9744479
23.97529728 29.4660957
```

```
 38.78227633 41.27265006]
```

This is the predicted response for known inputs. If you want predictions with new regressors, you can also apply .predict() with new data as the argument:

```
>>> x_new =
sm.add_constant(np.arange(10).reshape((-1, 2)))
>>> x_new
array([[1., 0., 1.],
       [1., 2., 3.],
       [1., 4., 5.],
       [1., 6., 7.],
       [1., 8., 9.]])

>>> y_new = results.predict(x_new)
>>> y_new
array([ 5.77760476,  7.18179502,  8.58598528,
9.99017554, 11.3943658 ])
```

You can notice that the predicted results are the same as those obtained with scikit-learn for the same problem.

Beyond Linear Regression

Linear regression is sometimes not appropriate, especially for nonlinear models of high complexity.

Fortunately, there are other regression techniques suitable for the cases where linear regression doesn't work well. Some of them are support vector machines, decision trees, random forest, and neural networks.

There are numerous Python libraries for regression using these techniques. Most of them are free and open-source. That's one of the reasons why Python is among the main programming languages for machine learning.

The package scikit-learn provides the means for using other regression techniques in a very similar way to what you've seen. It contains classes for support vector machines, decision trees, random forest, and more, with the methods .fit(), .predict(), .score(), and so on.

Clustering

Clustering is a set of techniques used to partition data into groups, or clusters. Clusters are loosely defined as groups of data objects that are more similar to other objects in their cluster than they are to data objects in other clusters.

What are clustering algorithms?

Clustering is an unsupervised machine learning task. You might also hear this referred to as cluster analysis because of the way this method works.

Using a clustering algorithm means you're going to give the algorithm a lot of input data with no labels and let it find any groupings in the data it can.

Those groupings are called *clusters*. A cluster is a group of data points that are similar to each other based on their relation to surrounding data points. Clustering is used for things like feature engineering or pattern discovery.

When you're starting with data you know nothing about,

clustering might be a good place to get some insight.

Types of clustering algorithms

There are different types of clustering algorithms that handle all kinds of unique data.

Density-based

In density-based clustering, data is grouped by areas of high concentrations of data points surrounded by areas of low concentrations of data points. Basically the algorithm finds the places that are dense with data points and calls those clusters.

The great thing about this is that the clusters can be any shape. You aren't constrained to expected conditions.

The clustering algorithms under this type don't try to assign outliers to clusters, so they get ignored.

Distribution-based

With a distribution-based clustering approach, all of the data points are considered parts of a cluster based on the probability that they belong to a given cluster.

It works like this: there is a center-point, and as the distance of a data point from the center increases, the probability of it being a part of that cluster decreases.

If you aren't sure of how the distribution in your data might be, you should consider a different type of algorithm.

Centroid-based

Centroid-based clustering is the one you probably hear about the most. It's a little sensitive to the initial parameters you give it, but it's fast and efficient.

These types of algorithms separate data points based on multiple centroids in the data. Each data point is assigned to a cluster based on its squared distance from the centroid.

This is the most commonly used type of clustering.

Hierarchical-based

Hierarchical-based clustering is typically used on hierarchical data, like you would get from a company database or taxonomies. It builds a tree of clusters so everything is organized from the top-down.

This is more restrictive than the other clustering types, but it's perfect for specific kinds of data sets.

When to use clustering

When you have a set of unlabeled data, it's very likely that you'll be using some kind of unsupervised learning algorithm.

There are a lot of different unsupervised learning techniques, like neural networks, reinforcement learning, and clustering. The specific type of algorithm you want to use is going to depend on what your data looks like.

You might want to use clustering when you're trying to do anomaly detection to try and find outliers in your data. It helps by finding those groups of clusters and showing the boundaries that would determine whether a data point is an outlier or not.

If you aren't sure of what features to use for your machine learning model, clustering discovers patterns you can use to figure out what stands out in the data.

Clustering is especially useful for exploring data you know nothing about. It might take some time to figure out which type of clustering algorithm works the best, but when you do, you'll get invaluable insight on your data. You might find connections you never would have thought of.

Some real world applications of clustering include fraud detection in insurance, categorizing books in a library, and customer segmentation in marketing. It can also be used in larger problems, like earthquake analysis or city planning.

The Top 8 Clustering Algorithms

Now that you have some background on how clustering algorithms work and the different types available, we can talk about the actual algorithms you'll commonly see in practice.

We'll implement these algorithms on an example data set from the sklearn library in Python.

We'll be using the *make_classification* data set from the sklearn library to demonstrate how different clustering algorithms aren't fit for all clustering problems.

K-means clustering algorithm

K-means clustering is the most commonly used clustering algorithm. It's a centroid-based algorithm and the simplest unsupervised learning algorithm.

This algorithm tries to minimize the variance of data points within a cluster. It's also how most people are introduced to unsupervised machine learning.

K-means is best used on smaller data sets because it iterates over *all* of the data points. That means it'll take more time to classify data points if there are a large amount of them in the data set.

Since this is how k-means clusters data points, it doesn't scale well.

Implementation:

```
from numpy import unique
from numpy import where
from matplotlib import pyplot
from sklearn.datasets import make_classification
```

```python
from sklearn.cluster import KMeans

# initialize the data set we'll work with
training_data, _ = make_classification(
    n_samples=1000,
    n_features=2,
    n_informative=2,
    n_redundant=0,
    n_clusters_per_class=1,
    random_state=4
)


# define the model
kmeans_model = KMeans(n_clusters=2)


# assign each data point to a cluster
dbscan_result =
dbscan_model.fit_predict(training_data)


# get all of the unique clusters
dbscan_clusters = unique(dbscan_result)


# plot the DBSCAN clusters
for dbscan_cluster in dbscan_clusters:
    # get data points that fall in this cluster
    index = where(dbscan_result == dbscan_clusters)
    # make the plot
    pyplot.scatter(training_data[index, 0],
    training_data[index, 1])


# show the DBSCAN plot
pyplot.show()
```

DBSCAN clustering algorithm

DBSCAN stands for density-based spatial clustering of applications with noise. It's a density-based clustering algorithm, unlike k-means.

This is a good algorithm for finding outliners in a data set. It finds arbitrarily shaped clusters based on the density of data points in different regions. It separates regions by areas of low-density so that it can detect outliers between the high-density clusters.

This algorithm is better than k-means when it comes to working with oddly shaped data.

DBSCAN uses two parameters to determine how clusters are defined: *minPts* (the minimum number of data points that need to be clustered together for an area to be considered high-density) and *eps* (the distance used to determine if a data point is in the same area as other data points).

Choosing the right initial parameters is critical for this algorithm to work.

Implementation:

```python
from numpy import unique
from numpy import where
from matplotlib import pyplot
from sklearn.datasets import make_classification
from sklearn.cluster import DBSCAN

# initialize the data set we'll work with
training_data, _ = make_classification(
    n_samples=1000,
```

```python
    n_features=2,
    n_informative=2,
    n_redundant=0,
    n_clusters_per_class=1,
    random_state=4
)


# define the model
dbscan_model = DBSCAN(eps=0.25, min_samples=9)


# train the model
dbscan_model.fit(training_data)


# assign each data point to a cluster
dbscan_result = dbscan_model.predict(training_data)


# get all of the unique clusters
dbscan_cluster = unique(dbscan_result)


# plot the DBSCAN clusters
for dbscan_cluster in dbscan_clusters:
    # get data points that fall in this cluster
    index = where(dbscan_result == dbscan_clusters)
    # make the plot
    pyplot.scatter(training_data[index, 0],
    training_data[index, 1])


# show the DBSCAN plot
pyplot.show()
```

Gaussian Mixture Model algorithm

One of the problems with k-means is that the data needs to
follow a circular format. The way k-means calculates the

distance between data points has to do with a circular path, so non-circular data isn't clustered correctly.

This is an issue that Gaussian mixture models fix. You don't need circular shaped data for it to work well.

The Gaussian mixture model uses multiple Gaussian distributions to fit arbitrarily shaped data.

There are several single Gaussian models that act as hidden layers in this hybrid model. So the model calculates the probability that a data point belongs to a specific Gaussian distribution and that's the cluster it will fall under.

Implementation:

```
from numpy import unique
from numpy import where
from matplotlib import pyplot
from sklearn.datasets import make_classification
from sklearn.mixture import GaussianMixture

# initialize the data set we'll work with
training_data, _ = make_classification(
    n_samples=1000,
    n_features=2,
    n_informative=2,
    n_redundant=0,
    n_clusters_per_class=1,
    random_state=4
)

# define the model
```

```python
gaussian_model = GaussianMixture(n_components=2)

# train the model
gaussian_model.fit(training_data)

# assign each data point to a cluster
gaussian_result =
gaussian_model.predict(training_data)

# get all of the unique clusters
gaussian_clusters = unique(gaussian_result)

# plot Gaussian Mixture the clusters
for gaussian_cluster in gaussian_clusters:
    # get data points that fall in this cluster
    index = where(gaussian_result ==
    gaussian_clusters)
    # make the plot
    pyplot.scatter(training_data[index, 0],
    training_data[index, 1])

# show the Gaussian Mixture plot
pyplot.show()
```

BIRCH algorithm

The Balance Iterative Reducing and Clustering using Hierarchies (BIRCH) algorithm works better on large data sets than the k-means algorithm.

It breaks the data into little summaries that are clustered instead of the original data points. The summaries hold as much distribution information about the data points as possible.

This algorithm is commonly used with other clustering algorithm because the other clustering techniques can be used on the summaries generated by BIRCH.

The main downside of the BIRCH algorithm is that it only works on numeric data values. You can't use this for categorical values unless you do some data transformations.

Implementation:

```python
from numpy import unique
from numpy import where
from matplotlib import pyplot
from sklearn.datasets import make_classification
from sklearn.cluster import Birch

# initialize the data set we'll work with
training_data, _ = make_classification(
    n_samples=1000,
    n_features=2,
    n_informative=2,
    n_redundant=0,
    n_clusters_per_class=1,
    random_state=4
)

# define the model
birch_model = Birch(threshold=0.03, n_clusters=2)

# train the model
birch_model.fit(training_data)

# assign each data point to a cluster
birch_result = birch_model.predict(training_data)
```

```python
# get all of the unique clusters
birch_clusters = unique(birch_result)

# plot the BIRCH clusters
for birch_cluster in birch_clusters:
    # get data points that fall in this cluster
    index = where(birch_result == birch_clusters)
    # make the plot
    pyplot.scatter(training_data[index, 0],
    training_data[index, 1])

# show the BIRCH plot
pyplot.show()
```

Affinity Propagation clustering algorithm

This clustering algorithm is completely different from the others in the way that it clusters data.

Each data point communicates with all of the other data points to let each other know how similar they are and that starts to reveal the clusters in the data. You don't have to tell this algorithm how many clusters to expect in the initialization parameters.

As messages are sent between data points, sets of data called *exemplars* are found and they represent the clusters.

An exemplar is found after the data points have passed messages to each other and form a consensus on what data point best represents a cluster.

When you aren't sure how many clusters to expect, like in a computer vision problem, this is a great algorithm to start with.

Implementation:

```python
from numpy import unique
from numpy import where
from matplotlib import pyplot
from sklearn.datasets import make_classification
from sklearn.cluster import AffinityPropagation

# initialize the data set we'll work with
training_data, _ = make_classification(
    n_samples=1000,
    n_features=2,
    n_informative=2,
    n_redundant=0,
    n_clusters_per_class=1,
    random_state=4
)

# define the model
model = AffinityPropagation(damping=0.7)

# train the model
model.fit(training_data)

# assign each data point to a cluster
result = model.predict(training_data)

# get all of the unique clusters
clusters = unique(result)

# plot the clusters
for cluster in clusters:
```

```
    # get data points that fall in this cluster
    index = where(result == cluster)
    # make the plot
    pyplot.scatter(training_data[index, 0],
    training_data[index, 1])

 # show the plot
 pyplot.show()
```

Mean-Shift clustering algorithm

This is another algorithm that is particularly useful for handling images and computer vision processing.

Mean-shift is similar to the BIRCH algorithm because it also finds clusters without an initial number of clusters being set.

This is a hierarchical clustering algorithm, but the downside is that it doesn't scale well when working with large data sets.

It works by iterating over all of the data points and shifts them towards the mode. The mode in this context is the high density area of data points in a region.

That's why you might hear this algorithm referred to as the mode-seeking algorithm. It will go through this iterative process with each data point and move them closer to where other data points are until all data points have been assigned to a cluster.

Implementation:

```python
from numpy import unique
from numpy import where
from matplotlib import pyplot
from sklearn.datasets import make_classification
from sklearn.cluster import MeanShift

# initialize the data set we'll work with
training_data, _ = make_classification(
    n_samples=1000,
    n_features=2,
    n_informative=2,
    n_redundant=0,
    n_clusters_per_class=1,
    random_state=4
)

# define the model
mean_model = MeanShift()

# assign each data point to a cluster
mean_result = mean_model.fit_predict(training_data)

# get all of the unique clusters
mean_clusters = unique(mean_result)

# plot Mean-Shift the clusters
for mean_cluster in mean_clusters:
    # get data points that fall in this cluster
    index = where(mean_result == mean_cluster)
    # make the plot
    pyplot.scatter(training_data[index, 0],
    training_data[index, 1])

# show the Mean-Shift plot
pyplot.show()
```

OPTICS algorithm

OPTICS stands for Ordering Points to Identify the Clustering Structure. It's a density-based algorithm similar to DBSCAN, but it's better because it can find meaningful clusters in data that varies in density. It does this by ordering the data points so that the closest points are neighbors in the ordering.

This makes it easier to detect different density clusters. The OPTICS algorithm only processes each data point once, similar to DBSCAN (although it runs slower than DBSCAN). There's also a special distance stored for each data point that indicates a point belongs to a specific cluster.

Implementation:

```python
from numpy import unique
from numpy import where
from matplotlib import pyplot
from sklearn.datasets import make_classification
from sklearn.cluster import OPTICS

# initialize the data set we'll work with
training_data, _ = make_classification(
    n_samples=1000,
    n_features=2,
    n_informative=2,
    n_redundant=0,
    n_clusters_per_class=1,
    random_state=4
)

# define the model
optics_model = OPTICS(eps=0.75, min_samples=10)

# assign each data point to a cluster
```

```
optics_result =
optics_model.fit_predict(training_data)

# get all of the unique clusters
optics_clusters = unique(optics_clusters)

# plot OPTICS the clusters
for optics_cluster in optics_clusters:
    # get data points that fall in this cluster
    index = where(optics_result == optics_clusters)
    # make the plot
    pyplot.scatter(training_data[index, 0],
    training_data[index, 1])

# show the OPTICS plot
pyplot.show()
```

Agglomerative Hierarchy clustering algorithm

This is the most common type of hierarchical clustering algorithm. It's used to group objects in clusters based on how similar they are to each other.

This is a form of bottom-up clustering, where each data point is assigned to its own cluster. Then those clusters get joined together.

At each iteration, similar clusters are merged until all of the data points are part of one big root cluster.

Agglomerative clustering is best at finding small clusters. The end result looks like a dendrogram so that you can easily visualize the clusters when the algorithm finishes.

Implementation:

```python
from numpy import unique
from numpy import where
from matplotlib import pyplot
from sklearn.datasets import make_classification
from sklearn.cluster import AgglomerativeClustering

# initialize the data set we'll work with
training_data, _ = make_classification(
    n_samples=1000,
    n_features=2,
    n_informative=2,
    n_redundant=0,
    n_clusters_per_class=1,
    random_state=4
)


# define the model
agglomerative_model =
AgglomerativeClustering(n_clusters=2)

# assign each data point to a cluster
agglomerative_result =
agglomerative_model.fit_predict(training_data)

# get all of the unique clusters
agglomerative_clusters = unique(agglomerative_result)

# plot the clusters
for agglomerative_cluster in agglomerative_clusters:
    # get data points that fall in this cluster
    index = where(agglomerative_result ==
    agglomerative_clusters)
    # make the plot
    pyplot.scatter(training_data[index, 0],
    training_data[index, 1])
```

```
# show the Agglomerative Hierarchy plot
pyplot.show()
```

Other types of clustering algorithms

We've covered eight of the top clustering algorithms, but there are plenty more than that available. There are some very specifically tuned clustering algorithms that quickly and precisely handle your data. Here are a few of the others that might be of interest to you.

There's another hierarchical algorithm that's the opposite of the agglomerative approach. It starts with a top-down clustering strategy. So it will start with one large root cluster and break out the individual clusters from there.

This is known as the **Divisive Hierarchical** clustering algorithm. There's research that shows this is creates more accurate hierarchies than agglomerative clustering, but it's way more complex.

Mini-Batch K-means is similar to K-means, except that it uses small random chunks of data of a fixed size so they can be stored in memory. This helps it run faster than K-means so it converges to a solution in less time.

The drawback to this algorithm is that the speed boost will cost you some cluster quality. The last algorithm we'll briefly cover is **Spectral Clustering**. This algorithm is completely different from the others we've looked at. It works by taking advantage of graph theory. This algorithm doesn't make any initial guesses about the clusters that are in the data set. It treats data points like nodes in a graph and clusters are found based on communities of nodes that have connecting edges.

K-means Algorithm

The k-means clustering method is machine learning technique used to identify clusters of data objects in a dataset. There are many different types of clustering methods, but k-means is one of the oldest and most approachable. These traits make implementing k-means clustering in Python reasonably straightforward, even for novice programmers and data scientists.

How to Perform K-Means Clustering in Python

In this section, you'll take a step-by-step tour of the conventional version of the k-means algorithm. Understanding the details of the algorithm is a fundamental step in the process of writing your k-means clustering pipeline in Python. What you learn in this section will help you decide if k-means is the right choice to solve your clustering problem.

Understanding the K-Means Algorithm

Conventional k-means requires only a few steps. The first step is to randomly select k centroids, where k is equal to the number of clusters you choose. Centroids are data points representing the center of a cluster.

The main element of the algorithm works by a two-step process called expectation-maximization. The expectation step assigns each data point to its nearest centroid. Then, the maximization step computes the mean of all the points for each cluster and sets the new centroid. Here's what the conventional version of the k-means algorithm looks like:

Algorithm 1 k-means algorithm

1: Specify the number k of clusters to assign.
2: Randomly initialize k centroids.
3: **repeat**
4:     **expectation:** Assign each point to its closest centroid.
5:     **maximization:** Compute the new centroid (mean) of each cluster.
6: **until** The centroid positions do not change.

The quality of the cluster assignments is determined by computing the sum of the squared error (SSE) after the centroids converge, or match the previous iteration's assignment. The SSE is defined as the sum of the squared Euclidean distances of each point to its closest centroid. Since this is a measure of error, the objective of k-means is to try to minimize this value.

The figure below shows the centroids and SSE updating through the first five iterations from two different runs of the k-means algorithm on the same dataset:

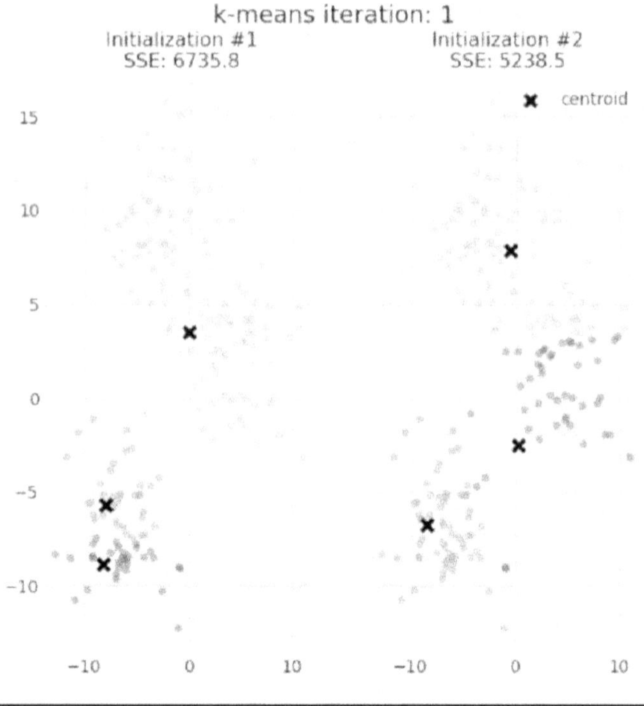

The purpose of this figure is to show that the initialization of the centroids is an important step. It also highlights the use of SSE as a measure of clustering performance. After choosing a number of clusters and the initial centroids, the expectation-maximization step is repeated until the centroid positions reach convergence and are unchanged.

The random initialization step causes the k-means algorithm to be nondeterministic, meaning that cluster assignments will vary if you run the same algorithm twice on the same dataset.

Researchers commonly run several initializations of the entire k-means algorithm and choose the cluster assignments from the initialization with the lowest SSE.

Writing Your First K-Means Clustering Code in Python

Thankfully, there's a robust implementation of k-means clustering in Python from the popular machine learning package scikit-learn. You'll learn how to write a practical implementation of the k-means algorithm using the scikit-learn version of the algorithm.

The code in this example requires some popular external Python packages and assumes that you've installed Python with Anaconda. For more information on setting up your Python environment for machine learning in Windows, read through Setting Up Python for Machine Learning on Windows.

Otherwise, you can begin by installing the required packages:

```
(base) $ conda install matplotlib numpy pandas
seaborn scikit-learn ipython
(base) $ conda install -c conda-forge kneed
```

The code is presented so that you can follow along in an ipython console or Jupyter Notebook. Click the prompt (»>) at the top right of each code block to see the code formatted for copy-paste. You can also download the source code used in this article by clicking on the link below:

This step will import the modules needed for all the code in this section:

```
In [1]: import matplotlib.pyplot as plt
   ...: from kneed import KneeLocator
   ...: from sklearn.datasets import make_blobs
   ...: from sklearn.cluster import KMeans
   ...: from sklearn.metrics import silhouette_score
   ...: from sklearn.preprocessing import
StandardScaler
```

You can generate the data from the above GIF using make_blobs(), a convenience function in scikit-learn used to generate synthetic clusters. make_blobs() uses these parameters:

- n_samples is the total number of samples to generate.
- centers is the number of centers to generate.
- cluster_std is the standard deviation.

make_blobs() returns a tuple of two values:

1. A two-dimensional NumPy array with the x- and y-values for each of the samples
2. A one-dimensional NumPy array containing the cluster labels for each sample

Generate the synthetic data and labels:

```
In [2]: features, true_labels = make_blobs(
   ...:        n_samples=200,
```

```
...:        centers=3,
...:        cluster_std=2.75,
...:        random_state=42
...: )
```

Nondeterministic machine learning algorithms like k-means are difficult to reproduce. The random_state parameter is set to an integer value so you can follow the data presented in the tutorial. In practice, it's best to leave random_state as the default value, None.

Here's a look at the first five elements for each of the variables returned by make_blobs():

```
In [3]: features[:5]
Out[3]:
array([[  9.77075874,    3.27621022],
       [ -9.71349666,   11.27451802],
       [ -6.91330582,   -9.34755911],
       [-10.86185913,  -10.75063497],
       [ -8.50038027,   -4.54370383]])

In [4]: true_labels[:5]
Out[4]: array([1, 0, 2, 2, 2])
```

Data sets usually contain numerical features that have been measured in different units, such as height (in inches) and weight (in pounds). A machine learning algorithm would consider weight more important than height only because the values for weight are larger and have higher variability from person to person.

Machine learning algorithms need to consider all features on an even playing field. That means the values for all features must be transformed to the same scale.

The process of transforming numerical features to use the same scale is known as feature scaling. It's an important data preprocessing step for most distance-based machine learning algorithms because it can have a significant impact on the performance of your algorithm.

There are several approaches to implementing feature scaling. A great way to determine which technique is appropriate for your dataset is to read scikit-learn's preprocessing documentation.

In this example, you'll use the StandardScaler class. This class implements a type of feature scaling called standardization. Standardization scales, or shifts, the values for each numerical feature in your dataset so that the features have a mean of 0 and standard deviation of 1:

```
In [5]: scaler = StandardScaler()
   ...: scaled_features =
   scaler.fit_transform(features)
```

Take a look at how the values have been scaled in scaled_features:

```
In [6]: scaled_features[:5]
Out[6]:
```

```
array([[ 2.13082109,  0.25604351],
       [-1.52698523,  1.41036744],
       [-1.00130152, -1.56583175],
       [-1.74256891, -1.76832509],
       [-1.29924521, -0.87253446]])
```

Now the data are ready to be clustered. The KMeans estimator class in scikit-learn is where you set the algorithm parameters before fitting the estimator to the data. The scikit-learn implementation is flexible, providing several parameters that can be tuned.

Here are the parameters used in this example:

- init controls the initialization technique. The standard version of the k-means algorithm is implemented by setting init to "random". Setting this to "k-means++" employs an advanced trick to speed up convergence, which you'll use later.
- n_clusters sets k for the clustering step. This is the most important parameter for k-means.
- n_init sets the number of initializations to perform. This is important because two runs can converge on different cluster assignments. The default behavior for the scikit-learn algorithm is to perform ten k-means runs and return the results of the one with the lowest SSE.
- max_iter sets the number of maximum iterations for each initialization of the k-means algorithm.

Instantiate the KMeans class with the following arguments:

```
In [7]: kmeans = KMeans(
   ...:         init="random",
   ...:         n_clusters=3,
   ...:         n_init=10,
   ...:         max_iter=300,
   ...:         random_state=42
   ...: )
```

The parameter names match the language that was used to describe the k-means algorithm earlier in the tutorial. Now that the k-means class is ready, the next step is to fit it to the data in scaled_features. This will perform ten runs of the k-means algorithm on your data with a maximum of 300 iterations per run:

```
In [8]: kmeans.fit(scaled_features)
Out[8]:
KMeans(init='random', n_clusters=3, random_state=42)
```

Statistics from the initialization run with the lowest SSE are available as attributes of kmeans after calling .fit():

```
In [9]: # The lowest SSE value
   ...: kmeans.inertia_
Out[9]: 74.57960106819854

In [10]: # Final locations of the centroid
   ...: kmeans.cluster_centers_
Out[10]:
array([[ 1.19539276,  0.13158148],
       [-0.25813925,  1.05589975],
       [-0.91941183, -1.18551732]])
```

```
In [11]: # The number of iterations required to
converge
    ...: kmeans.n_iter_
Out[11]: 6
```

Finally, the cluster assignments are stored as a one-dimensional NumPy array in kmeans.labels_. Here's a look at the first five predicted labels:

```
In [12]: kmeans.labels_[:5]
Out[12]: array([0, 1, 2, 2, 2], dtype=int32)
```

Note that the order of the cluster labels for the first two data objects was flipped. The order was [1, 0] in true_labels but [0, 1] in kmeans.labels_ even though those data objects are still members of their original clusters in kmeans.lables_.

This behavior is normal, as the ordering of cluster labels is dependent on the initialization. Cluster 0 from the first run could be labeled cluster 1 in the second run and vice versa. This doesn't affect clustering evaluation metrics.

Choosing the Appropriate Number of Clusters

In this section, you'll look at two methods that are commonly used to evaluate the appropriate number of clusters:

1. The elbow method
2. The silhouette coefficient

These are often used as complementary evaluation techniques rather than one being preferred over the other. To perform the elbow method, run several k-means, increment k with each iteration, and record the SSE:

```
In [13]: kmeans_kwargs = {
    ...:         "init": "random",
    ...:         "n_init": 10,
    ...:         "max_iter": 300,
    ...:         "random_state": 42,
    ...: }
    ...:
    ...: # A list holds the SSE values for each k
    ...: sse = []
    ...: for k in range(1, 11):
    ...:         kmeans = KMeans(n_clusters=k,
**kmeans_kwargs)
    ...:         kmeans.fit(scaled_features)
    ...:         sse.append(kmeans.inertia_)
```

The previous code block made use of Python's dictionary unpacking operator (**). To learn more about this powerful Python operator, check out How to Iterate Through a Dictionary in Python.

When you plot SSE as a function of the number of clusters, notice that SSE continues to decrease as you increase k. As more centroids are added, the distance from each point to its closest centroid will decrease.

There's a sweet spot where the SSE curve starts to bend known as the elbow point. The x-value of this point is thought to be a reasonable trade-off between error and number of clusters.

In this example, the elbow is located at x=3:

```
In [14]:  plt.style.use("fivethirtyeight")
   ...:  plt.plot(range(1, 11), sse)
   ...:  plt.xticks(range(1, 11))
   ...:  plt.xlabel("Number of Clusters")
   ...:  plt.ylabel("SSE")
   ...:  plt.show()
```

The above code produces the following plot:

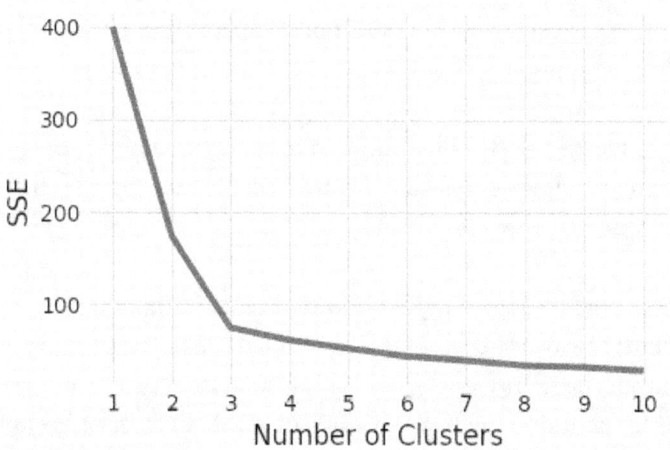

Determining the elbow point in the SSE curve isn't always straightforward. If you're having trouble choosing the elbow point of the curve, then you could use a Python package, kneed, to identify the elbow point programmatically:

```
In [15]: kl = KneeLocator(
   ...:         range(1, 11), sse, curve="convex",
```

```
        direction="decreasing"
    ...: )

 In [16]: kl.elbow
 Out[16]: 3
```

The silhouette coefficient is a measure of cluster cohesion and separation. It quantifies how well a data point fits into its assigned cluster based on two factors:

1. How close the data point is to other points in the cluster
2. How far away the data point is from points in other clusters

Silhouette coefficient values range between -1 and 1. Larger numbers indicate that samples are closer to their clusters than they are to other clusters.

In the scikit-learn implementation of the silhouette coefficient, the average silhouette coefficient of all the samples is summarized into one score. The silhouette score() function needs a minimum of two clusters, or it will raise an exception.

Loop through values of k again. This time, instead of computing SSE, compute the silhouette coefficient:

```
 In [17]: # A list holds the silhouette coefficients
 for each k
    ...: silhouette_coefficients = []
    ...:
    ...: # Notice you start at 2 clusters for
```

```
   silhouette coefficient
   ...: for k in range(2, 11):
   ...:      kmeans = KMeans(n_clusters=k,
**kmeans_kwargs)
   ...:         kmeans.fit(scaled_features)
   ...:         score =
silhouette_score(scaled_features, kmeans.labels_)
   ...:         silhouette_coefficients.append(score)
```

Plotting the average silhouette scores for each k shows that
the best choice for k is 3 since it has the maximum score:

```
In [18]: plt.style.use("fivethirtyeight")
   ...: plt.plot(range(2, 11),
silhouette_coefficients)
   ...: plt.xticks(range(2, 11))
   ...: plt.xlabel("Number of Clusters")
   ...: plt.ylabel("Silhouette Coefficient")
   ...: plt.show()
```

The above code produces the following plot:

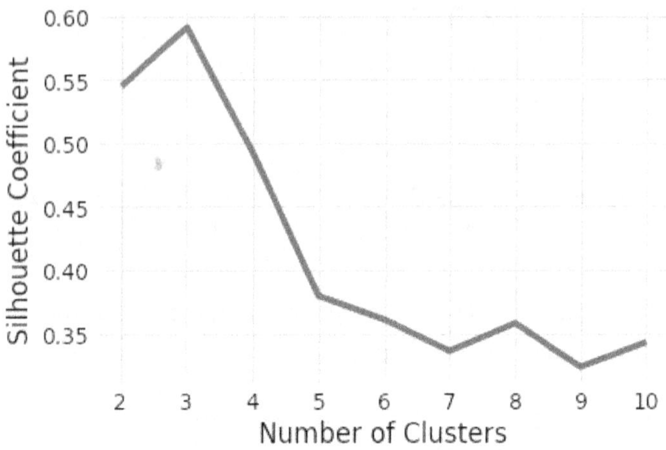

Ultimately, your decision on the number of clusters to use should be guided by a combination of domain knowledge and clustering evaluation metrics.

Evaluating Clustering Performance Using Advanced Techniques

The elbow method and silhouette coefficient evaluate clustering performance without the use of ground truth labels. Ground truth labels categorize data points into groups based on assignment by a human or an existing algorithm. These types of metrics do their best to suggest the correct number of clusters but can be deceiving when used without context.

When comparing k-means against a density-based approach on nonspherical clusters, the results from the elbow method and silhouette coefficient rarely match human intuition. This scenario highlights why advanced clustering evaluation techniques are necessary. To visualize an example, import these additional modules:

```
In [19]: from sklearn.cluster import DBSCAN
    ...: from sklearn.datasets import make_moons
    ...: from sklearn.metrics import
adjusted_rand_score
```

This time, use make_moons() to generate synthetic data in the shape of crescents:

```
In [20]: features, true_labels = make_moons(
    ...:         n_samples=250, noise=0.05,
random_state=42
    ...: )
    ...: scaled_features =
scaler.fit_transform(features)
```

Fit both a k-means and a DBSCAN algorithm to the new data and visually assess the performance by plotting the cluster assignments with Matplotlib:

```
In [21]: # Instantiate k-means and dbscan algorithms
    ...: kmeans = KMeans(n_clusters=2)
    ...: dbscan = DBSCAN(eps=0.3)
    ...:
    ...: # Fit the algorithms to the features
    ...: kmeans.fit(scaled_features)
    ...: dbscan.fit(scaled_features)
    ...:
    ...: # Compute the silhouette scores for each
algorithm
    ...: kmeans_silhouette = silhouette_score(
    ...:         scaled_features, kmeans.labels_
```

```
...: ).round(2)
...: dbscan_silhouette = silhouette_score(
...:     scaled_features, dbscan.labels_
...: ).round (2)
```

Print the silhouette coefficient for each of the two algorithms and compare them. A higher silhouette coefficient suggests better clusters, which is misleading in this scenario:

```
In [22]: kmeans_silhouette
Out[22]: 0.5

In [23]: dbscan_silhouette
Out[23]: 0.38
```

The silhouette coefficient is higher for the k-means algorithm. The DBSCAN algorithm appears to find more natural clusters according to the shape of the data:

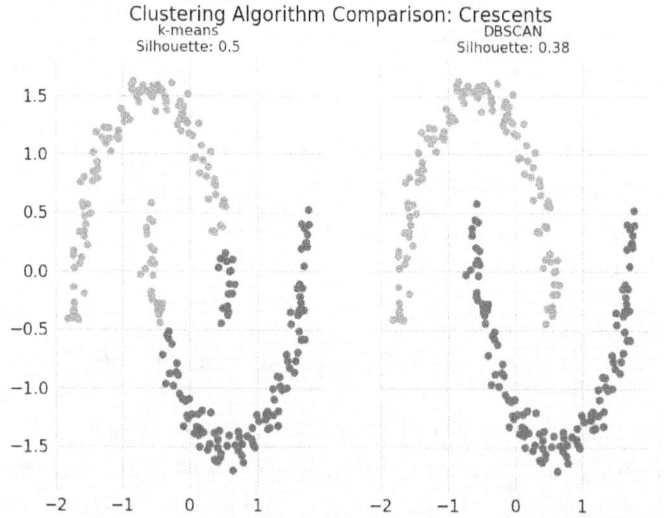

This suggests that you need a better method to compare the performance of these two clustering algorithms.

Compare the clustering results of DBSCAN and k-means using ARI as the performance metric:

```
In [25]: ari_kmeans =
adjusted_rand_score(true_labels, kmeans.labels_)
    ...: ari_dbscan =
    adjusted_rand_score(true_labels, dbscan.labels_)

In [26]: round(ari_kmeans, 2)
Out[26]: 0.47

In [27]: round(ari_dbscan, 2)
Out[27]: 1.0
```

The ARI output values range between -1 and 1. A score close to 0.0 indicates random assignments, and a score close to 1 indicates perfectly labeled clusters.

Based on the above output, you can see that the silhouette coefficient was misleading. ARI shows that DBSCAN is the best choice for the synthetic crescents example as compared to k-means.

How to Build a K-Means Clustering Pipeline in Python

Now that you have a basic understanding of k-means clustering in Python, it's time to perform k-means clustering on a real-world dataset. These data contain gene expression values from a manuscript authored by The Cancer Genome Atlas (TCGA) Pan-Cancer analysis project investigators.

There are 881 samples (rows) representing five distinct cancer subtypes. Each sample has gene expression values for 20,531 genes (columns). The dataset is available from the UC Irvine Machine Learning Repository, but you can use the Python code below to obtain the data programmatically.

In this section, you'll build a robust k-means clustering pipeline. Since you'll perform multiple transformations of the original input data, your pipeline will also serve as a practical clustering framework.

Building a K-Means Clustering Pipeline

Assuming you want to start with a fresh namespace, import

all the modules needed to build and evaluate the pipeline, including pandas and seaborn for more advanced visualizations:

```
In [1]: import tarfile
   ...: import urllib
   ...:
   ...: import numpy as np
   ...: import matplotlib.pyplot as plt
   ...: import pandas as pd
   ...: import seaborn as sns
   ...:
   ...: from sklearn.cluster import KMeans
   ...: from sklearn.decomposition import PCA
   ...: from sklearn.metrics import
silhouette_score, adjusted_rand_score
   ...: from sklearn.pipeline import Pipeline
   ...: from sklearn.preprocessing import
LabelEncoder, MinMaxScaler
```

Download and extract the TCGA dataset from UCI:

```
In [2]: uci_tcga_url =
"https://archive.ics.uci.edu/ml/machine-learning-databases/0040
   ...: archive_name =
"TCGA-PANCAN-HiSeq-801x20531.tar.gz"

   ...: # Build the url
   ...: full_download_url =
urllib.parse.urljoin(uci_tcga_url, archive_name)
   ...:
   ...: # Download the file
   ...: r = urllib.request.urlretrieve
(full_download_url, archive_name)

   ...: # Extract the data from the archive
   ...: tar = tarfile.open(archive_name, "r:gz")
```

```
...: tar.extractall()
...: tar.close()
```

After the download and extraction is completed, you should have a directory that looks like this:

```
TCGA-PANCAN-HiSeq-801x20531/
|  |————————
                  |————————
  data.csv
  labels.csv
```

The KMeans class in scikit-learn requires a NumPy array as an argument. The NumPy package has a helper function to load the data from the text file into memory as NumPy arrays:

```
In [3]: datafile =
"TCGA-PANCAN-HiSeq-801x20531/data.csv"
    ...: labels_file =
    "TCGA-PANCAN-HiSeq-801x20531/labels.csv"
    ...:
    ...: data = np.genfromtxt(
    ...:     datafile,
    ...:     delimiter=",",
    ...:     usecols=range(1, 20532),
    ...:     skip_header=1
    ...: )
    ...:
    ...: true_label_names = np.genfromtxt(
    ...:     labels_file,
    ...:     delimiter=",",
    ...:     usecols=(1,),
    ...:     skip_header=1,
    ...:     dtype="str"
    ...: )
```

Check out the first three columns of data for the first five samples as well as the labels for the first five samples:

```
In [4]: data[:5, :3]
Out[4]:
array([[0.         , 2.01720929, 3.26552691],
       [0.         , 0.59273209, 1.58842082],
       [0.         , 3.51175898, 4.32719872],
       [0.         , 3.66361787, 4.50764878],
       [0.         , 2.65574107, 2.82154696]])


In [5]: true_label_names[:5]
Out[5]: array(['PRAD', 'LUAD', 'PRAD', 'PRAD',
'BRCA'], dtype='<U4')
```

The data variable contains all the gene expression values from 20,531 genes. The true_label_names are the cancer types for each of the 881 samples. The first record in data corresponds with the first label in true_labels.

The labels are strings containing abbreviations of cancer types:

- BRCA: Breast invasive carcinoma
- COAD: Colon adenocarcinoma
- KIRC: Kidney renal clear cell carcinoma
- LUAD: Lung adenocarcinoma
- PRAD: Prostate adenocarcinoma

To use these labels in the evaluation methods, you first need to convert the abbreviations to integers with LabelEncoder:

```
In [6]: label_encoder = LabelEncoder()

In [7]: true_labels =
label_encoder.fit_transform(true_label_names)

In [8]: true_labels[:5]
Out[8]: array([4, 3, 4, 4, 0])
```

Since the label_encoder has been fitted to the data, you can see the unique classes represented using .classes_. Store the length of the array to the variable n_clusters for later use:

```
In [9]: label_encoder.classes_
Out[9]: array(['BRCA', 'COAD', 'KIRC', 'LUAD',
'PRAD'], dtype='<U4')

In [10]: n_clusters = len(label_encoder.classes_)
```

In practical machine learning pipelines, it's common for the data to undergo multiple sequences of transformations before it feeds into a clustering algorithm. You learned about the importance of one of these transformation steps, feature scaling, earlier in this tutorial. An equally important data transformation technique is dimensionality reduction, which reduces the number of features in the dataset by either removing or combining them.

Dimensionality reduction techniques help to address a problem with machine learning algorithms known as the curse of dimensionality. In short, as the number of features increases, the feature space becomes sparse. This sparsity makes it difficult for algorithms to find data objects near one another in higher-dimensional space. Since the gene expression dataset has over 20,000 features, it qualifies as a great candidate for dimensionality reduction.

Principal Component Analysis (PCA) is one of many dimensionality reduction techniques. PCA transforms the input data by projecting it into a lower number of dimensions called components. The components capture the variability of the input data through a linear combination of the input data's features.

Note: A full description of PCA is out of scope for this tutorial, but you can learn more about it in the scikit-learn user guide.

The next code block introduces you to the concept of scikit-learn pipelines. The scikit-learn Pipeline class is a concrete implementation of the abstract idea of a machine learning pipeline.

Your gene expression data aren't in the optimal format for the KMeans class, so you'll need to build a preprocessing pipeline. The pipeline will implement an alternative to the StandardScaler class called MinMaxScaler for feature scaling. You use MinMaxScaler when you *do not* assume that the shape of all your features follows a normal distribution.

The next step in your preprocessing pipeline will implement the PCA class to perform dimensionality reduction:

```
In [11]: preprocessor = Pipeline(
    ...:     [
    ...:             ("scaler", MinMaxScaler()),
    ...:             ("pca", PCA(n_components=2,
    random_state=42)),
    ...:     ]
    ...: )
```

Now that you've built a pipeline to process the data, you'll build a separate pipeline to perform k-means clustering. You'll override the following default arguments of the KMeans class:

- init: You'll use "k-means++" instead of "random" to ensure centroids are initialized with some distance between them. In most cases, this will be an improvement over "random".
- n_init: You'll increase the number of initializations to ensure you find a stable solution.
- max_iter: You'll increase the number of iterations per initialization to ensure that k-means will converge.

Build the k-means clustering pipeline with user-defined arguments in the KMeans constructor:

```
In [12]: clusterer = Pipeline(
    ...:     [
    ...:             (
    ...:                 "kmeans",
    ...:                 KMeans(
    ...:                     n_clusters=n_clusters,
    ...:                     init="k-means++",
```

```
   ...:                              n_init=50,
   ...:                              max_iter=500,
   ...:                              random_state=42,
   ...:                  ),
   ...:              ),
   ...:          ]
   ...:  )
```

The Pipeline class can be chained to form a larger pipeline. Build an end-to-end k-means clustering pipeline by passing the "preprocessor" and "clusterer" pipelines to Pipeline:

```
In [13]: pipe = Pipeline(
   ...:       [
   ...:           ("preprocessor", preprocessor),
   ...:           ("clusterer", clusterer)
   ...:       ]
   ...:  )
```

Calling .fit() with data as the argument performs all the pipeline steps on the data:

```
In [14]: pipe.fit(data)
Out[14]:
Pipeline(steps=[('preprocessor',
                 Pipeline(steps=[('scaler',
                 MinMaxScaler()),
                                 ('pca',
                                  PCA(n_components=2,
                                  random_state=42))])),
                ('clusterer',
                 Pipeline(steps=[('kmeans',
                                  KMeans(max_iter=500,
                                  n_clusters=5,
```

```
                                        n_init=50,
                                          random_state=42))]
```

The pipeline performs all the necessary steps to execute k-means clustering on the gene expression data! Depending on your Python REPL, .fit() may print a summary of the pipeline. Objects defined inside pipelines are accessible using their step name.

Evaluate the performance by calculating the silhouette coefficient:

```
In [15]: preprocessed_data =
pipe["preprocessor"].transform(data)

In [16]: predicted_labels =
pipe["clusterer"]["kmeans"].labels_

In [17]: silhouette_score(preprocessed_data,
predicted_labels)
Out[17]: 0.51187755284503304
```

Calculate ARI, too, since the ground truth cluster labels are available:

```
In [18]: adjusted_rand_score(true_labels,
predicted_labels)
Out[18]: 0.722276752060253
```

As mentioned earlier, the scale for each of these clustering performance metrics ranges from -1 to 1. A silhouette coefficient of 0 indicates that clusters are significantly overlapping one another, and a silhouette coefficient of 1 indicates clusters are well-separated. An ARI score of 0 indicates that cluster labels are randomly assigned, and an ARI score of 1 means that the true labels and predicted labels form identical clusters.

Since you specified n_components=2 in the PCA step of the k-means clustering pipeline, you can also visualize the data in the context of the true labels and predicted labels. Plot the results using a pandas DataFrame and the seaborn plotting library:

```
In [19]: pcadf = pd.DataFrame(
    ...:         pipe["preprocessor"].transform(data),
    ...:         columns=["component_1", "component_2"],
    ...: )
    ...:
    ...: pcadf["predicted_cluster"] =
pipe["clusterer"]["kmeans"].labels_
    ...: pcadf["true_label"] =
label_encoder.inverse_transform(true_labels)

In [20]: plt.style.use("fivethirtyeight")
    ...: plt.figure(figsize=(8, 8))
    ...:
    ...: scat = sns.scatterplot(
    ...:         "component_1",
    ...:         "component_2",
    ...:         s=50,
    ...:         data=pcadf,
    ...:         hue="predicted_cluster",
    ...:         style="true_label",
    ...:         palette="Set2",
    ...: )
    ...:
    ...: scat.set_title(
```

```
...:        "Clustering results from TCGA
Pan-Cancer\nGene Expression Data"
...: )
...: plt.legend(bbox_to_anchor=(1.05, 1), loc=2,
borderaxespad=0.0)
...:
...: plt.show()
```

Here's what the plot looks like:

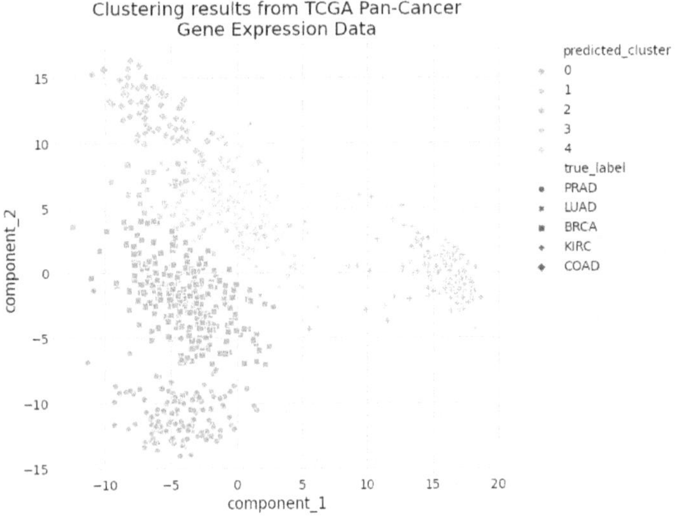

The visual representation of the clusters confirms the results
of the two clustering evaluation metrics. The performance
of your pipeline was pretty good. The clusters only slightly
overlapped, and cluster assignments were much better than
random.

Tuning a K-Means Clustering Pipeline

Your first k-means clustering pipeline performed well, but there's still room to improve. That's why you went through the trouble of building the pipeline: you can tune the parameters to get the most desirable clustering results.

The process of parameter tuning consists of sequentially altering one of the input values of the algorithm's parameters and recording the results. At the end of the parameter tuning process, you'll have a set of performance scores, one for each new value of a given parameter. Parameter tuning is a powerful method to maximize performance from your clustering pipeline.

By setting the PCA parameter n_components=2, you squished all the features into two components, or dimensions. This value was convenient for visualization on a two-dimensional plot. But using only two components means that the PCA step won't capture all of the explained variance of the input data.

Explained variance measures the discrepancy between the PCA-transformed data and the actual input data. The relationship between n_components and explained variance can be visualized in a plot to show you how many components you need in your PCA to capture a certain percentage of the variance in the input data. You can also use clustering performance metrics to evaluate how many components are necessary to achieve satisfactory clustering results.

In this example, you'll use clustering performance metrics to identify the appropriate number of components in the PCA step. The Pipeline class is powerful in this situation. It allows you to perform basic parameter tuning using a for loop.

Iterate over a range of n_components and record evaluation metrics for each iteration:

```
In [21]: # Empty lists to hold evaluation metrics
    ...: silhouette_scores = []
    ...: ari_scores = []
    ...: for n in range(2, 11):
    ...:         # This set the number of components for
    pca,
    ...:         # but leaves other steps unchanged
    ...:         pipe["preprocessor"]["pca"].n_components
    = n
    ...:         pipe.fit(data)
    ...:
    ...:         silhouette_coef = silhouette_score(
    ...:             pipe["preprocessor"].transform(data),
    ...:             pipe["clusterer"]["kmeans"].labels_,
    ...:         )
    ...:         ari = adjusted_rand_score(
    ...:             true_labels,
    ...:             pipe["clusterer"]["kmeans"].labels_,
    ...:         )
    ...:
    ...:         # Add metrics to their lists
    ...:         silhouette_scores.append(silhouette_coef)
    ...:         ari_scores.append(ari)
```

Plot the evaluation metrics as a function of n_components to visualize the relationship between adding components and the performance of the k-means clustering results:

```
In [22]: plt.style.use("fivethirtyeight")
    ...: plt.figure(figsize=(6, 6))
    ...: plt.plot(
    ...:         range(2, 11),
    ...:         silhouette_scores,
    ...:         c="#008fd5",
    ...:         label="Silhouette Coefficient",
    ...: )
    ...: plt.plot(range(2, 11), ari_scores,
    c="#fc4f30", label="ARI")
    ...:
    ...: plt.xlabel("n_components")
    ...: plt.legend()
    ...: plt.title("Clustering Performance as a
    Function of n_components")
    ...: plt.tight_layout()
    ...: plt.show()
```

The above code generates the a plot showing performance
metrics as a function of n_components:

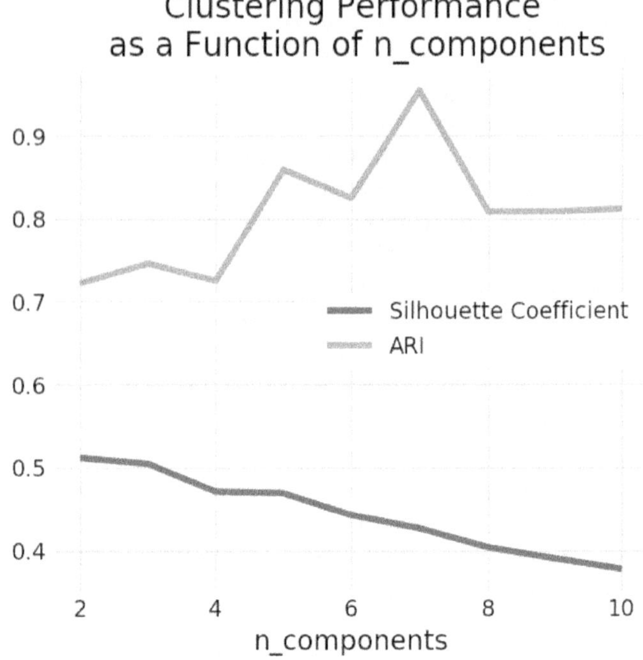

There are two takeaways from this figure:

- The silhouette coefficient decreases linearly. The silhouette coefficient depends on the distance between points, so as the number of dimensions increases, the sparsity increases.
- The ARI improves significantly as you add components. It appears to start tapering off after n_components=7, so that would be the value to use for presenting the best clustering results from this pipeline.

Like most machine learning decisions, you must balance optimizing clustering evaluation metrics with the goal of the clustering task. In situations when cluster labels are available, as is the case with the cancer dataset used in this tutorial, ARI is a reasonable choice. ARI quantifies how accurately your pipeline was able to reassign the cluster labels.

The silhouette coefficient, on the other hand, is a good choice for exploratory clustering because it helps to identify sub-clusters. These subclusters warrant additional investigation, which can lead to new and important insights.

Mean Shift Algorithm

In this chapter, we begin building our own mean shift algorithm from scratch. I will add one more cluster/group to the original data. Feel free to add the new data or leave it the same as it was.

```python
import matplotlib.pyplot as plt
from matplotlib import style
style.use('ggplot')
import numpy as np

X = np.array([[1, 2],
              [1.5, 1.8],
              [5, 8 ],
              [8, 8],
              [1, 0.6],
              [9,11],
              [8,2],
              [10,2],
              [9,3],])

plt.scatter(X[:,0], X[:,1], s=150)
plt.show()

colors = 10*["g","r","c","b","k"]
```

If ran, the code generates:

Just like in the K Means part, this creates obvious groups. With K Means, we even told the machine that we wanted 'k' clusters (2). With Mean Shift, we're expecting that the machine just figures that out on its own, and, for us, we're expecting three groups with the code above.

We will begin our Mean Shift class:

```python
class Mean_Shift:
    def __init__(self, radius=4):
        self.radius = radius
```

We will start with a radius of 4, since we can estimate with our dataset that a radius of four makes sense. That's all we need for now in the initialization method. Moving on to the fit method:

```python
def fit(self, data):
        centroids = {}

        for i in range(len(data)):
            centroids[i] = data[i]
```

Here, we begin with creating starting centroids. Recall the method for Mean Shift is:

- Make all datapoints centroids
- Take mean of all featuresets within centroid's radius, setting this mean as new centroid.
- Repeat step #2 until convergence.

So far we have done step 1. Now we need to repeat step 2 until convergence!

```python
while True:
            new_centroids = []
            for i in centroids:
                in_bandwidth = []
                centroid = centroids[i]
                for featureset in data:
                    if
                    np.linalg.norm(featureset-centroid)
                    < self.radius:
                        in_bandwidth.append(featureset)

                new_centroid =
                np.average(in_bandwidth,axis=0)
                new_centroids.append(tuple(new_centroid))

            uniques =
```

```
sorted(list(set(new_centroids)))
```

Here, we begin iterating through each centroid, and finding all featuresets in range. From there, we are taking the average, and setting that average as the "new centroid." Finally, we're creating a uniques variable, which tracks the sorted list of all known centroids. We use set here since there may be duplicates, and duplicate centroids are really just the same centroid.

To conclude the fit method:

```python
prev_centroids = dict(centroids)

        centroids = {}
        for i in range(len(uniques)):
            centroids[i] = np.array(uniques[i])

        optimized = True

        for i in centroids:
            if not np.array_equal(centroids[i],
            prev_centroids[i]):
                optimized = False
            if not optimized:
                break

        if optimized:
            break

    self.centroids = centroids
```

Here we note the previous centroids, before we begin to reset "current" or "new" centroids by setting them as the uniques.

Finally, we compare the previous centroids to the new ones, and measure movement. If any of the centroids have moved, then we're not content that we've got full convergence and optimization, and we want to go ahead and run another cycle. If we are optimized, great, we break, and then finally set the centroids attribute to the final centroids we came up with.

We can now wrap up this first part, and the class, adding the following:

```
clf = Mean_Shift()
clf.fit(X)

centroids = clf.centroids

plt.scatter(X[:,0], X[:,1], s=150)

for c in centroids:
    plt.scatter(centroids[c][0], centroids[c][1],
    color='k', marker='*', s=150)

plt.show()
```

Full code up to this point:

```python
import matplotlib.pyplot as plt
from matplotlib import style
style.use('ggplot')
import numpy as np

X = np.array([[1, 2],
              [1.5, 1.8],
              [5, 8 ],
              [8, 8],
              [1, 0.6],
              [9,11],
              [8,2],
              [10,2],
              [9,3],])

##plt.scatter(X[:,0], X[:,1], s=150)
##plt.show()

colors = 10*["g","r","c","b","k"]
```

```python
class Mean_Shift:
    def __init__(self, radius=4):
        self.radius = radius

    def fit(self, data):
        centroids = {}

        for i in range(len(data)):
            centroids[i] = data[i]

        while True:
            new_centroids = []
            for i in centroids:
                in_bandwidth = []
                centroid = centroids[i]
                for featureset in data:
                    if
                    np.linalg.norm(featureset-centroid)
                    < self.radius:
                        in_bandwidth.append(featureset)

                new_centroid =
                np.average(in_bandwidth,axis=0)
                new_centroids.append(tuple(new_centroid))

            uniques =
            sorted(list(set(new_centroids)))

            prev_centroids = dict(centroids)

            centroids = {}
            for i in range(len(uniques)):
                centroids[i] = np.array(uniques[i])

            optimized = True
```

```python
        for i in centroids:
            if not np.array_equal(centroids[i],
            prev_centroids[i]):
                optimized = False
            if not optimized:
                break

        if optimized:
            break

    self.centroids = centroids


clf = Mean_Shift()
clf.fit(X)

centroids = clf.centroids

plt.scatter(X[:,0], X[:,1], s=150)

for c in centroids:
    plt.scatter(centroids[c][0], centroids[c][1],
    color='k', marker='*', s=150)

plt.show()
```

At this point, we've got the centroids we need, and we're
feeling pretty smart. From here, all we need to do is calculate the Euclidean distances, and we have our clusters and
classifications! Predictions are easy from there! There's just
one problem: The radius

We've basically hard-coded the radius. I did it by looking at the
dataset and deciding 4 was a good number. It's not dynamic

at all. Imagine if we had 50 dimensions? It wouldn't be so simple. Can a machine look at the dataset and come up with something decent?

Our code up to this point:

```python
import matplotlib.pyplot as plt
from matplotlib import style
style.use('ggplot')
import numpy as np

X = np.array([[1, 2],
              [1.5, 1.8],
              [5, 8 ],
              [8, 8],
              [1, 0.6],
              [9,11],
              [8,2],
              [10,2],
              [9,3],])

##plt.scatter(X[:,0], X[:,1], s=150)
##plt.show()

colors = 10*["g","r","c","b","k"]

class Mean_Shift:
    def __init__(self, radius=4):
        self.radius = radius

    def fit(self, data):
        centroids = {}

        for i in range(len(data)):
            centroids[i] = data[i]
```

```python
while True:
    new_centroids = []
    for i in centroids:
        in_bandwidth = []
        centroid = centroids[i]
        for featureset in data:
            if
            np.linalg.norm(featureset-centroid)
            < self.radius:
                in_bandwidth.append(featureset)

        new_centroid =
        np.average(in_bandwidth,axis=0)
        new_centroids.append(tuple(new_centroid))

    uniques =
    sorted(list(set(new_centroids)))

    prev_centroids = dict(centroids)

    centroids = {}
    for i in range(len(uniques)):
        centroids[i] = np.array(uniques[i])

    optimized = True

    for i in centroids:
        if not np.array_equal(centroids[i],
        prev_centroids[i]):
            optimized = False
        if not optimized:
            break

    if optimized:
        break

self.centroids = centroids
```

```python
clf = Mean_Shift()
clf.fit(X)

centroids = clf.centroids

plt.scatter(X[:,0], X[:,1], s=150)

for c in centroids:
    plt.scatter(centroids[c][0], centroids[c][1],
    color='k', marker='*', s=150)

plt.show()
```

The code works, but we decided that the hard-coded radius is weak. We want something better! First, I will begin by modifying our ___init____ method:

```python
def __init__(self, radius=None, radius_norm_step =
100):
        self.radius = radius
        self.radius_norm_step = radius_norm_step
```

So the plan here is to create a massive radius, but make that radius go in steps, like bandwidths, or a bunch of radiuses with different lengths, which we'll call steps. If a featureset is in the closest radius, it will have a much higher "weight" than one much further away. The only question is what those steps ought to be! Now, beginning our fit method:

```python
def fit(self, data):

        if self.radius == None:
            all_data_centroid = np.average(data,
            axis=0)
            all_data_norm =
            np.linalg.norm(all_data_centroid)
            self.radius = all_data_norm /
            self.radius_norm_step

        centroids = {}

        for i in range(len(data)):
            centroids[i] = data[i]
```

Here, if the user hasn't hard-coded the radius, then we're going to find the "center" of ALL of the data. Then, we will take the norm of that data, then we say each radius with self.radius is basically the full data-length, divided by how many steps we wanted to have. From here the centroids definitions remain the same as before in the above code. Now we begin the optimization while loop:

```python
weights = [i for i in
range(self.radius_norm_step)][::-1]
        while True:
            new_centroids = []
            for i in centroids:
                in_bandwidth = []
                centroid = centroids[i]

                for featureset in data:
                    #if
                    np.linalg.norm(featureset-centroid)
```

```
                < self.radius:
                #
                in_bandwidth.append(featureset)
                distance =
                np.linalg.norm(featureset-centroid)
                if distance == 0:
                    distance = 0.00000000001
                weight_index =
                int(distance/self.radius)
                if weight_index >
                self.radius_norm_step-1:
                    weight_index =
                    self.radius_norm_step-1

                to_add =
                (weights[weight_index]**2)*[featureset
                in_bandwidth +=to_add


            new_centroid =
            np.average(in_bandwidth,axis=0)
            new_centroids.append(tuple(new_centroid))

        uniques =
        sorted(list(set(new_centroids)))
```

Notice the definition of weights, and then the change within the for featureset in data. The weights list is just a simple list that we'll take how many "radius steps" a featureset is from the centroid, take those # of steps, treating them as index values for the weight list. Iterating through the features, we calculate distances, add weights, then add the "weighted" number of centroids to the in_bandwidth. When all done, we take the average of in_bandwidth, making that the new centroid.

Note that this weighting method is very cumbersome. There are better ways to do it, I am sure. This is simply what I came up with quickly, feel free to improve. With this method, however, it is highly likely that we have centroids that are extremely close, but not identical. We want to merge these too. For that, we do:

```python
to_pop = []

                for i in uniques:
                    for ii in [i for i in uniques]:
                        if i == ii:
                            pass
                        elif
                        np.linalg.norm(np.array(i)-np.array(ii))
                        <= self.radius:
                            #print(np.array(i),
                            np.array(ii))
                            to_pop.append(ii)
                            break

                for i in to_pop:
                    try:
                        uniques.remove(i)
                    except:
                        pass
```

Again, this isn't elegance, but it will work. We continue along with code that was already here from the previous tutorial:

```python
prev_centroids = dict(centroids)
                centroids = {}
                for i in range(len(uniques)):
                    centroids[i] = np.array(uniques[i])
```

```
        optimized = True

        for i in centroids:
            if not np.array_equal(centroids[i],
            prev_centroids[i]):
                optimized = False

        if optimized:
            break


    self.centroids = centroids
```

Now, however, we kind of expect "fit" to also classify the existing featuresets. Let's add that in, still working within the fit method:

```
 self.classifications = {}

        for i in range(len(self.centroids)):
            self.classifications[i] = []

        for featureset in data:
            #compare distance to either centroid
            distances =
            [np.linalg.norm(featureset-self.centroids[centr
            for centroid in self.centroids]
            #print(distances)
            classification =
            (distances.index(min(distances)))

            # featureset that belongs to that cluster
            self.classifications[classification].append(fea
```

All this does is take known featuresets, and calculate the minimum distance to the centroids, and classify as belonging to the closest centroid. Finally, we can take this code and also create a predict method as well:

```
def predict(self,data):
        #compare distance to either centroid
        distances =
        [np.linalg.norm(data-self.centroids[centroid])
        for centroid in self.centroids]
        classification =
        (distances.index(min(distances)))
        return classification
```

Great, the rest of the code stays the same at the end, but I will still put it here:

```
clf = Mean_Shift()
clf.fit(X)

centroids = clf.centroids
print(centroids)

colors = 10*['r','g','b','c','k','y']

for classification in clf.classifications:
    color = colors[classification]
    for featureset in
    clf.classifications[classification]:
        plt.scatter(featureset[0],featureset[1],
        marker = "x", color=color, s=150, linewidths
        = 5, zorder = 10)

for c in centroids:
```

```
    plt.scatter(centroids[c][0],centroids[c][1],
    color='k', marker = "*", s=150, linewidths = 5)

plt.show()
```

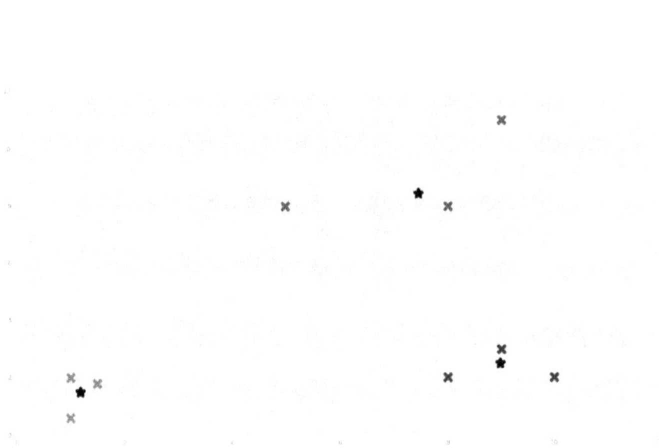

Awesome! We can put our clustering algorithm through a real stress test with Scikit-Learn's make_blobs, which we can use to create featuresets.

At the top of the script, you can do:

```
from sklearn.datasets.samples_generator import
make_blobs
```

Then for our featuresets:

```
X, y = make_blobs(n_samples=15, centers=3,
n_features=2)
```

Make sure you delete or comment out the previous definition for X.

Full code up to this point:

```python
import matplotlib.pyplot as plt
from matplotlib import style
import numpy as np
from sklearn.datasets.samples_generator import make_blobs

style.use('ggplot')

X, y = make_blobs(n_samples=15, centers=3,
n_features=2)
##X = np.array([[1, 2],
##              [1.5, 1.8],
##              [5, 8],
##              [8, 8],
##              [1, 0.6],
##              [9, 11],
##              [8, 2],
##              [10, 2],
##              [9, 3]])


##plt.scatter(X[:, 0],X[:, 1], marker = "x", s=150,
linewidths = 5, zorder = 10)
##plt.show()

'''

1. Start at every datapoint as a cluster center

2. take mean of radius around cluster, setting that
as new cluster center
```

```
3. Repeat #2 until convergence.

'''

class Mean_Shift:
    def __init__(self, radius = None,
    radius_norm_step = 100):
        self.radius = radius
        self.radius_norm_step = radius_norm_step


    def fit(self,data):

        if self.radius == None:
            all_data_centroid =
            np.average(data,axis=0)
            all_data_norm =
            np.linalg.norm(all_data_centroid)
            self.radius =
            all_data_norm/self.radius_norm_step
            print(self.radius)

        centroids = {}

        for i in range(len(data)):
            centroids[i] = data[i]

        weights = [i for i in
        range(self.radius_norm_step)][::-1]
        while True:
            new_centroids = []
            for i in centroids:
                in_bandwidth = []
                centroid = centroids[i]

                for featureset in data:

                    distance =
                    np.linalg.norm(featureset-centroid)
```

```python
                if distance == 0:
                    distance = 0.00000000001
                weight_index =
                int(distance/self.radius)
                if weight_index >
                self.radius_norm_step-1:
                    weight_index =
                    self.radius_norm_step-1

                to_add =
                (weights[weight_index]**2)*[featureset]
                in_bandwidth +=to_add

            new_centroid =
            np.average(in_bandwidth,axis=0)
            new_centroids.append(tuple(new_centroid))

    uniques =
    sorted(list(set(new_centroids)))

    to_pop = []

    for i in uniques:
        for ii in [i for i in uniques]:
            if i == ii:
                pass
        elif
        np.linalg.norm(np.array(i)-np.array(ii))
        <= self.radius:
                #print(np.array(i),
                np.array(ii))
                to_pop.append(ii)
                break

    for i in to_pop:
        try:
            uniques.remove(i)
```

```python
        except:
            pass

    prev_centroids = dict(centroids)
    centroids = {}
    for i in range(len(uniques)):
        centroids[i] = np.array(uniques[i])

    optimized = True

    for i in centroids:
        if not np.array_equal(centroids[i],
        prev_centroids[i]):
            optimized = False

    if optimized:
        break

self.centroids = centroids
self.classifications = {}

for i in range(len(self.centroids)):
    self.classifications[i] = []

for featureset in data:
    #compare distance to either centroid
    distances =
    [np.linalg.norm(featureset-self.centroids[centr
    for centroid in self.centroids]
    #print(distances)
    classification =
    (distances.index(min(distances)))

    # featureset that belongs to that cluster
    self.classifications[classification].append(fea
```

```python
    def predict(self,data):
        #compare distance to either centroid
        distances =
        [np.linalg.norm(data-self.centroids[centroid])
        for centroid in self.centroids]
        classification =
        (distances.index(min(distances)))
        return classification


clf = Mean_Shift()
clf.fit(X)

centroids = clf.centroids
print(centroids)

colors = 10*['r','g','b','c','k','y']

for classification in clf.classifications:
    color = colors[classification]
    for featureset in
    clf.classifications[classification]:
        plt.scatter(featureset[0],featureset[1],
        marker = "x", color=color, s=150, linewidths
        = 5, zorder = 10)

for c in centroids:
    plt.scatter(centroids[c][0],centroids[c][1],
    color='k', marker = "*", s=150, linewidths = 5)

plt.show()
```

Hierarchical Clustering

Hierarchical clustering is another unsupervised learning algorithm that is used to group together the unlabeled data points having similar characteristics. Hierarchical clustering algorithms falls into following two categories:

Agglomerative hierarchical algorithms: In agglomerative hierarchical algorithms, each data point is treated as a single cluster and then successively merge or agglomerate (bottom-up approach) the pairs of clusters. The hierarchy of the clusters is represented as a dendrogram or tree structure.

Divisive hierarchical algorithms: On the other hand, in divisive hierarchical algorithms, all the data points are treated as one big cluster and the process of clustering involves dividing (Top-down approach) the one big cluster into various small clusters.

Steps to Perform Agglomerative Hierarchical Clustering

We are going to explain the most used and important Hierarchical clustering i.e. agglomerative. The steps to perform the same is as follows:

- **Step 1:** Treat each data point as single cluster. Hence, we will be having, say K clusters at start. The number of data points will also be K at start.
- **Step 2:** Now, in this step we need to form a big cluster by joining two closet datapoints. This will result in total of K-1 clusters.
- **Step 3:** Now, to form more clusters we need to join two closet clusters. This will result in total of K-2 clusters.
- **Step 4:** Now, to form one big cluster repeat the above three steps until K would become 0 i.e. no more data points left to join.
- **Step 5:** At last, after making one single big cluster, dendrograms will be used to divide into multiple clusters depending upon the problem.

Role of Dendrograms in Agglomerative Hierarchical Clustering

As we discussed in the last step, the role of dendrogram starts once the big cluster is formed. Dendrogram will be used to split the clusters into multiple cluster of related data points depending upon our problem. It can be understood with the help of following example:

Example 1

To understand, let us start with importing the required libraries as follows:

```
%matplotlib inline
import matplotlib.pyplot as plt
import numpy as np
```

Next, we will be plotting the datapoints we have taken for this example:

```
X =
np.array([[7,8],[12,20],[17,19],[26,15],[32,37],[87,75],[73,85
[62,80],[73,60],[87,96],])
labels = range(1, 11) plt.figure(figsize=(10, 7))
plt.subplots_adjust(bottom=0.1)
plt.scatter(X[:,0],X[:,1], label='True Position')
for label, x, y in zip(labels, X[:, 0], X[:, 1]):
plt.annotate(label,xy=(x, y), xytext=(-3,
3),textcoords='offset points', ha='right',
va='bottom')
plt.show()
```

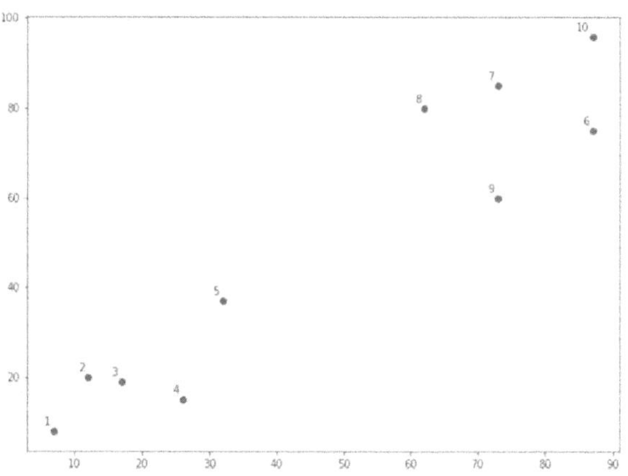

From the above diagram, it is very easy to see that we have two clusters in out datapoints but in the real world data, there can be thousands of clusters. Next, we will be plotting the dendrograms of our datapoints by using **Scipy** library:

```
from scipy.cluster.hierarchy import dendrogram,
linkage frommatplotlib import pyplot as plt
linked = linkage(X, 'single')
labelList = range(1, 11)
plt.figure(figsize=(10, 7))
dendrogram(linked,
orientation='top',labels=labelList,
distance_sort='descending',show_leaf_counts=True)
plt.show()
```

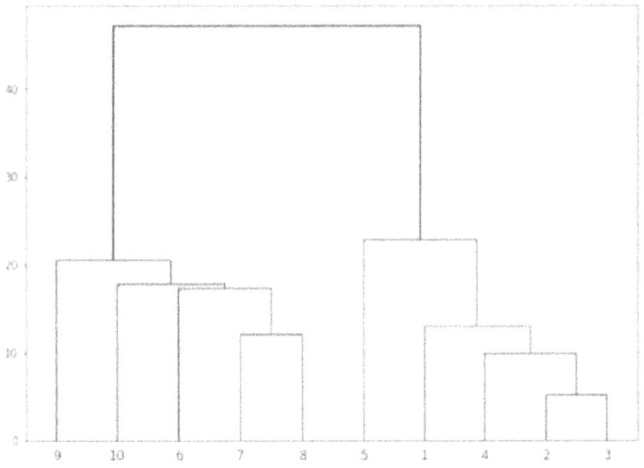

Now, once the big cluster is formed, the longest vertical distance is selected. A vertical line is then drawn through it as shown in the following diagram. As the horizontal line crosses the blue line at two points, the number of clusters would be two.

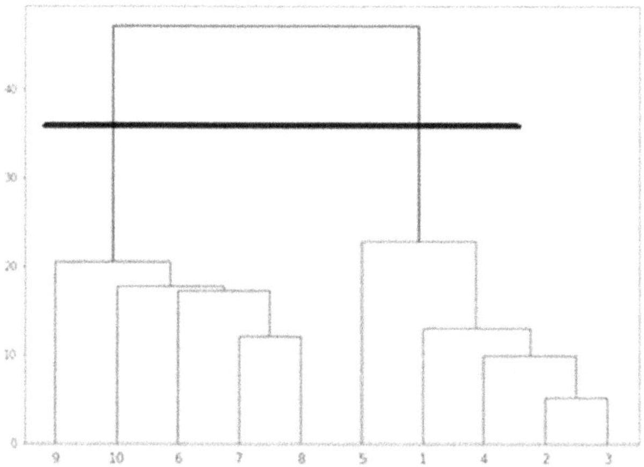

Next, we need to import the class for clustering and call its **fit_predict** method to predict the cluster. We are importing **AgglomerativeClustering** class of **sklearn.cluster** library:

```
from sklearn.cluster import AgglomerativeClustering
cluster = AgglomerativeClustering(n_clusters=2,
affinity='euclidean', linkage='ward')
cluster.fit_predict(X)
```

Next, plot the cluster with the help of following code:

```
plt.scatter(X[:,0],X[:,1], c=cluster.labels_,
cmap='rainbow')
```

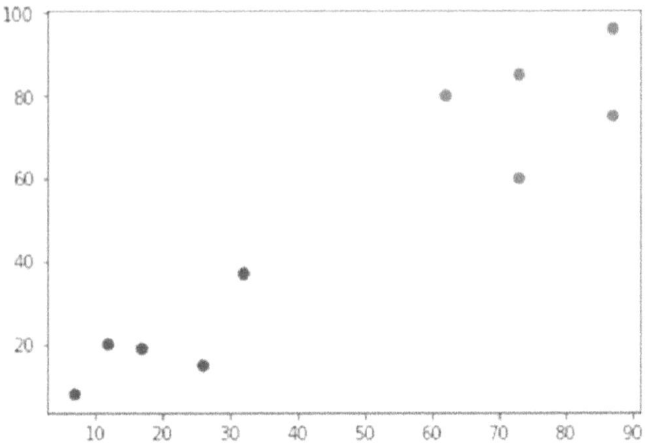

The above diagram shows the two clusters from our data-points.

Example 2

As we understood the concept of dendrograms from the simple example discussed above, let us move to another example in which we are creating clusters of the data point in Pima Indian Diabetes Dataset by using hierarchical clustering:

```python
import matplotlib.pyplot as plt import pandas as pd
%matplotlib inline import numpy as np
from pandas import read_csv
path = r"C:\pima-indians-diabetes.csv"
headernames = ['preg', 'plas', 'pres', 'skin',
'test', 'mass', 'pedi', 'age',
'class']
data = read_csv(path, names=headernames)
array = data.values
```

```
X = array[:,0:8]
Y = array[:,8] data.shape (768, 9)
data.head()
```

	preg	Plas	Pres	skin	test	mass	pedi	age	class
0	6	148	72	35	0	33.6	0.627	50	1
1	1	85	66	29	0	26.6	0.351	31	0
2	8	183	64	0	0	23.3	0.672	32	1
3	1	89	66	23	94	28.1	0.167	21	0
4	0	137	40	35	168	43.1	2.288	33	1

```
patient_data = data.iloc[:, 3:5].values import
scipy.cluster.hierarchyas shc
plt.figure(figsize=(10, 7)) plt.title("Patient
Dendograms")
dend = shc.dendrogram(shc.linkage(data,
method='ward'))
```

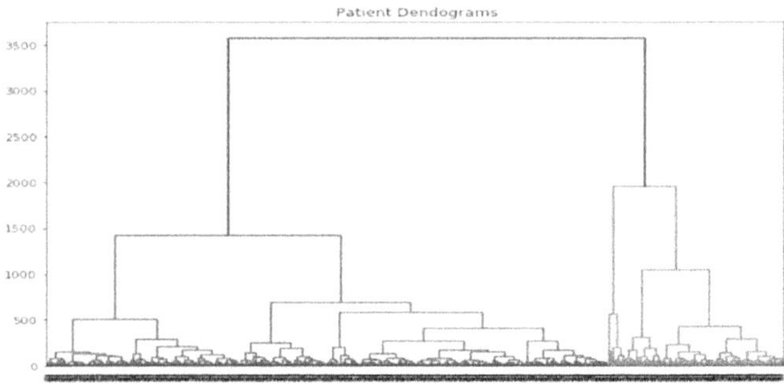

```
from sklearn.cluster import AgglomerativeClustering
cluster = AgglomerativeClustering(n_clusters=4,
affinity='euclidean', linkage='ward')
cluster.fit_predict(patient_data)
plt.figure(figsize=(10, 7))
plt.scatter(patient_data[:,0], patient_data[:,1],
c=cluster.labels_, cmap='rainbow')
```

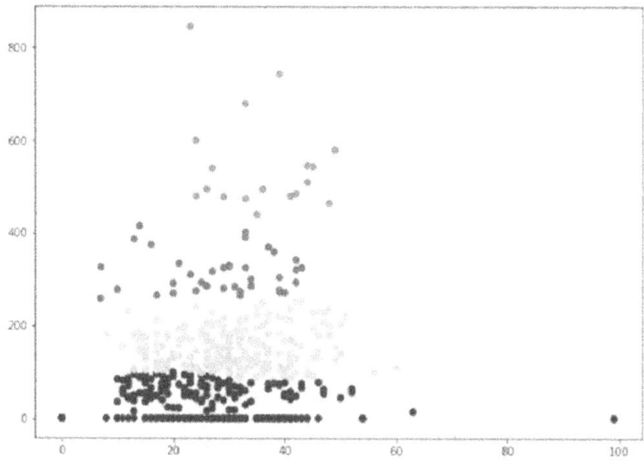

Finding Nearest Neighbors

K-nearest neighbors (KNN) algorithm is a type of supervised ML algorithm which can be used for both classification as well as regression predictive problems. However, it is mainly used for classification predictive problems in industry. The following two properties would define KNN well:

- **Lazy learning algorithm:** KNN is a lazy learning algorithm because it does not have a specialized training phase and uses all the data for training while classification.
- **Non-parametric learning algorithm:** KNN is also a non-parametric learning algorithm because it doesn't assume anything about the underlying data.

Working of KNN Algorithm

K-nearest neighbors (KNN) algorithm uses 'feature similarity' to predict the values of new data points which further means that the new data point will be assigned a value based on how closely it matches the points in the training set. We can understand its working with the help of following steps:

- **Step 1:** For implementing any algorithm, we need dataset.

So during the first step of KNN, we must load the training as well as test data.

- **Step 2:** Next, we need to choose the value of K i.e. the nearest data points. K can be any integer.
- **Step 3:** For each point in the test data do the following:

3.1: Calculate the distance between test data and each row of training data with the help of any of the method namely: Euclidean, Manhattan or Hamming distance. The most commonly used method to calculate distance is Euclidean.

3.2: Now, based on the distance value, sort them in ascending order.

3.3: Next, it will choose the top K rows from the sorted array.

3.4: Now, it will assign a class to the test point based on most frequent class of these rows.

Step 4: End

Example

The following is an example to understand the concept of K and working of KNN algorithm: Suppose we have a dataset which can be plotted as follows:

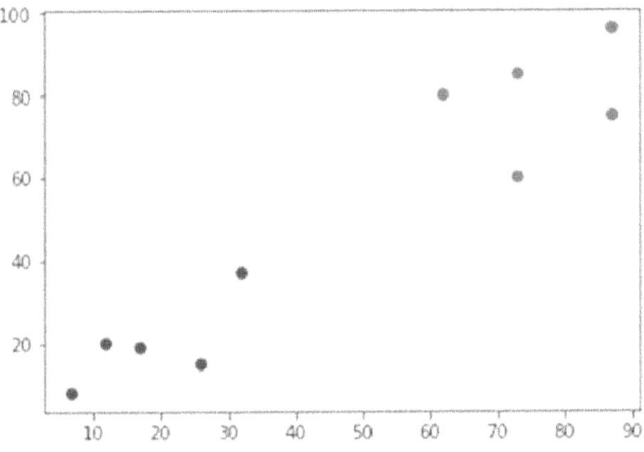

Now, we need to classify new data point with black dot (at point 60,60) into blue or red class. We are assuming K = 3 i.e. it would find three nearest data points. It is shown in the next diagram:

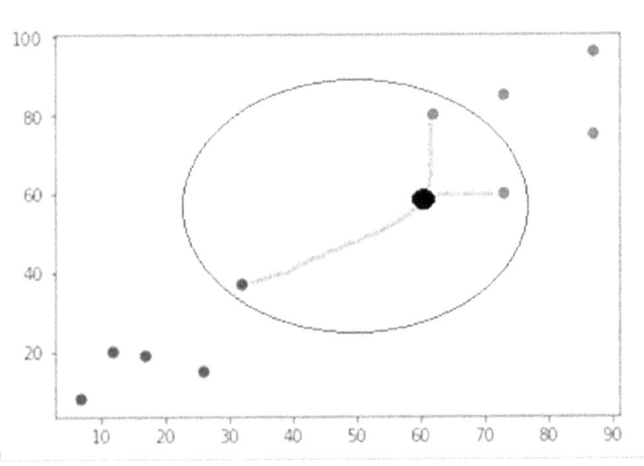

We can see in the above diagram the three nearest neighbors of the data point with black dot. Among those three, two of them lies in Red class hence the black dot will also be assigned in red class.

Implementation in Python

As we know K-nearest neighbors (KNN) algorithm can be used for both classification as well as regression. The following are the recipes in Python to use KNN as classifier as well as regressor:

KNN as Classifier

First, start with importing necessary python packages:

```
import numpy as np
import matplotlib.pyplot as plt import pandas as pd
Next, download the iris dataset from its weblink as
follows:
path =
"https://archive.ics.uci.edu/ml/machine-learning-
databases/iris/iris.data"
```

Next, we need to assign column names to the dataset as follows:

```
headernames = ['sepal-length','sepal-width',
'petal-length', 'petal-width',
'Class']
```

Now, we need to read dataset to pandas dataframe as follows:

```
dataset = pd.read_csv(path, names=headernames)
dataset.head()
```

	sepal-length	sepal-width	petal-length	petal-width	Class
0	5.1	3.5	1.4	0.2	Iris-setosa
1	4.9	3.0	1.4	0.2	Iris-setosa
2	4.7	3.2	1.3	0.2	Iris-setosa
3	4.6	3.1	1.5	0.2	Iris-setosa
4	5.0	3.6	1.4	0.2	Iris-setosa

Data Preprocessing will be done with the help of following script lines:

```
X = dataset.iloc[:, :-1].values y = dataset.iloc[:, 4].values
```

Next, we will divide the data into train and test split. Following code will split the dataset into 60% training data and 40% of testing data:

```
from sklearn.model_selectionimport train_test_split
X_train, X_test, y_train, y_test = train_test_split(X, y, test_size=0.40)
```

Next, data scaling will be done as follows:

```
from sklearn.preprocessing import StandardScaler
scaler = StandardScaler()
```

```
scaler.fit(X_train)
X_train = scaler.transform(X_train)
X_test = scaler.transform(X_test)
```

Next, train the model with the help of KNeighborsClassifier class of sklearn as follows:

```
from sklearn.neighbors import KNeighborsClassifier
classifier = KNeighborsClassifier(n_neighbors=8)
classifier.fit(X_train, y_train)
```

At last we need to make prediction. It can be done with the help of following script:

```
y_pred = classifier.predict(X_test)
```

Next, print the results as follows:

```
from sklearn.metrics import classification_report,
confusion_matrix, accuracy_score
result = confusion_matrix(y_test, y_pred)
print("Confusion Matrix:")
print(result)
result1 = classification_report(y_test, y_pred)
print("Classification Report:",)
print (result1)
result2 = accuracy_score(y_test,y_pred)
print("Accuracy:",result2)
```

Output

```
Confusion Matrix:
[[21  0  0]
 [ 0 16  0]
 [ 0  7 16]]
Classification Report:
                precision    recall  f1-score   support

    Iris-setosa      1.00      1.00      1.00        21
 Iris-versicolor     0.70      1.00      0.82        16
  Iris-virginica     1.00      0.70      0.82        23


      micro avg      0.88      0.88      0.88        60
      macro avg      0.90      0.90      0.88        60
   weighted avg      0.92      0.88      0.88        60
```

```
Accuracy: 0.88333333333333333
```

KNN as Regressor

First, start with importing necessary Python packages:

```
import numpy as np import pandas as pd
```

Next, download the iris dataset from its weblink as follows:

```
path =
"https://archive.ics.uci.edu/ml/machine-learning-
databases/iris/iris.data"
```

Next, we need to assign column names to the dataset as follows:

```
headernames = ['sepal-length','sepal-width',
'petal-length', 'petal-width',
'Class']
```

Now, we need to read dataset to pandas dataframe as follows:

```
data = pd.read_csv(url, names=headernames)
array = data.values
X = array[:,:2] Y = array[:,2] data.shape
output:(150, 5)
Next, import KNeighborsRegressor from sklearn to fit
the model:
from sklearn.neighbors import KNeighborsRegressor
knnr= KNeighborsRegressor(n_neighbors=10)
knnr.fit(X, y)
```

At last, we can find the MSE as follows:

```
print ("The MSE
is:",format(np.power(y-knnr.predict(X),2).mean()))
```

Output

```
The MSE is: 0.12226666666666669
```

Pros and Cons of KNN

Pros

- It is very simple algorithm to understand and interpret.
- It is very useful for nonlinear data because there is no

assumption about data in this algorithm.
- It is a versatile algorithm as we can use it for classification as well as regression.
- It has relatively high accuracy but there are much better supervised learning models than KNN.

Cons

- It is computationally a bit expensive algorithm because it stores all the training data.
- High memory storage required as compared to other supervised learning algorithms.
- Prediction is slow in case of big N.
- It is very sensitive to the scale of data as well as irrelevant features.

Applications of KNN

The following are some of the areas in which KNN can be applied successfully:

Banking System

KNN can be used in banking system to predict weather an individual is fit for loan approval? Does that individual have the characteristics similar to the defaulters one?

Calculating Credit Ratings

KNN algorithms can be used to find an individual's credit rating by comparing with the persons having similar traits.

Politics

With the help of KNN algorithms, we can classify a potential voter into various classes like "Will Vote", "Will not Vote", "Will Vote to Party 'Congress', "Will Vote to Party 'BJP'.

Other areas in which KNN algorithm can be used are Speech Recognition, Handwriting Detection, Image Recognition and Video Recognition.

Performance Metrics

There are various metrics which we can use to evaluate the performance of ML algorithms, classification as well as regression algorithms. We must carefully choose the metrics for evaluating ML performance because –

- How the performance of ML algorithms is measured and compared will be dependent entirely on the metric you choose.
- How you weight the importance of various characteristics in the result will be influenced completely by the metric you choose.

Performance Metrics for Classification Problems

We have discussed classification and its algorithms in the previous chapters. Here, we are going to discuss various performance metrics that can be used to evaluate predictions for classification problems.

Confusion Matrix

It is the easiest way to measure the performance of a classification problem where the output can be of two or more type of classes. A confusion matrix is nothing but a table with two dimensions viz. "Actual" and "Predicted" and furthermore, both the dimensions have "True Positives (TP)", "True Negatives (TN)", "False Positives (FP)", "False Negatives (FN)" as shown below –

Actual

	1	0
1	True Positives (TP)	False Positives (FP)
0		True Negatives (TN)

Predicted

Explanation of the terms associated with confusion matrix are as follows –

- **True Positives (TP)** – It is the case when both actual class & predicted class of data point is 1.
- **True Negatives (TN)** – It is the case when both actual class & predicted class of data point is 0.
- **False Positives (FP)** – It is the case when actual class of data point is 0 & predicted class of data point is 1.
- **False Negatives (FN)** – It is the case when actual class of data point is 1 & predicted class of data point is 0.

We can use confusion_matrix function of sklearn.metrics to

compute Confusion Matrix of our classification model.

Classification Accuracy

It is most common performance metric for classification algorithms. It may be defined as the number of correct predictions made as a ratio of all predictions made. We can easily calculate it by confusion matrix with the help of following formula –

$$Accuracy = \frac{TP + TN}{TP + FP + FN + TN}$$

We can use accuracy_score function of sklearn.metrics to compute accuracy of our classification model.

Classification Report

This report consists of the scores of Precisions, Recall, F1 and Support. They are explained as follows –

Precision

Precision, used in document retrievals, may be defined as the number of correct documents returned by our ML model. We can easily calculate it by confusion matrix with the help of following formula –

$$Precision = \frac{TP}{TP + FP}$$

Recall or Sensitivity

Recall may be defined as the number of positives returned by our ML model. We can easily calculate it by confusion matrix with the help of following formula –

$$Recall = \frac{TP}{TP + FN}$$

Specificity

Specificity, in contrast to recall, may be defined as the number of negatives returned by our ML model. We can easily calculate it by confusion matrix with the help of following formula –

$$Specificity = \frac{TN}{TN + FP}$$

Support

Support may be defined as the number of samples of the true response that lies in each class of target values.

F1 Score

This score will give us the harmonic mean of precision and recall. Mathematically, F1 score is the weighted average of the precision and recall. The best value of F1 would be 1 and worst would be 0. We can calculate F1 score with the help of following formula –

$$F1$$
$$= 2*precision \quad (*recall) \ / \ precision(+ recall)$$

F1 score is having equal relative contribution of precision and recall. We can use classification_report function of sklearn.metrics to get the classification report of our classification model.

AUC (Area Under ROC curve)

AUC (Area Under Curve)-ROC (Receiver Operating Character-istic) is a performance metric, based on varying threshold values, for classification problems. As name suggests, ROC is a probability curve and AUC measure the separability. In simple words, AUC-ROC metric will tell us about the capability of model in distinguishing the classes. Higher the AUC, better the model.

Mathematically, it can be created by plotting TPR (True Positive Rate) i.e. Sensitivity or recall vs FPR (False Positive Rate) i.e. 1-Specificity, at various threshold values. Following is the graph showing ROC, AUC having TPR at y-axis and FPR at x-axis –

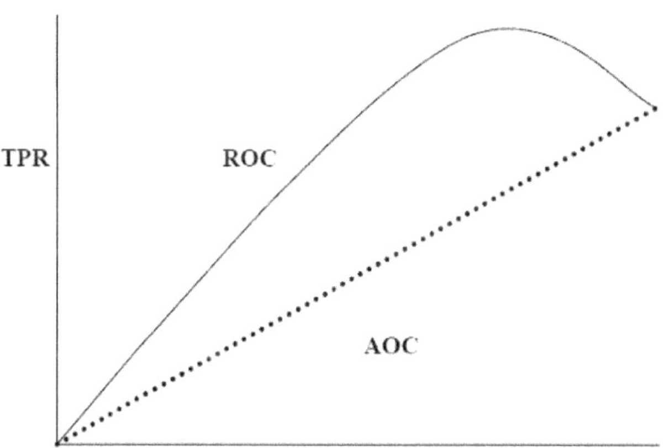

We can use roc_auc_score function of sklearn.metrics to compute AUC-ROC.

LOGLOSS (Logarithmic Loss)

It is also called Logistic regression loss or cross-entropy loss. It basically defined on probability estimates and measures the performance of a classification model where the input is a probability value between 0 and 1. It can be understood more clearly by differentiating it with accuracy. As we know that accuracy is the count of predictions (predicted value = actual value) in our model whereas Log Loss is the amount of uncertainty of our prediction based on how much it varies from the actual label. With the help of Log Loss value, we can have more accurate view of the performance of our model. We can use log_loss function of sklearn.metrics to compute Log Loss.

Example

The following is a simple recipe in Python which will give us an insight about how we can use the above explained performance metrics on binary classification model –

```python
from sklearn.metrics import confusion_matrix
from sklearn.metrics import accuracy_score
from sklearn.metrics import classification_report
from sklearn.metrics import roc_auc_score
from sklearn.metrics import log_loss
X_actual = [1, 1, 0, 1, 0, 0, 1, 0, 0, 0]
Y_predic = [1, 0, 1, 1, 1, 0, 1, 1, 0, 0]
results = confusion_matrix(X_actual, Y_predic)
print ('Confusion Matrix :')
print(results)
print ('Accuracy Score is',accuracy_score(X_actual,
```

```
Y_predic))
print ('Classification Report : ')
print (classification_report(X_actual, Y_predic))
print('AUC-ROC:',roc_auc_score(X_actual, Y_predic))
print('LOGLOSS Value is',log_loss(X_actual,
Y_predic))
```

Output

```
Confusion Matrix :
[
   [3 3]
   [1 3]
]
Accuracy Score is 0.6
Classification Report :
              precision      recall      f1-score
                  support
       0        0.75         0.50        0.60
       6
       1        0.50         0.75        0.60
       4
micro avg       0.60         0.60        0.60
10
macro avg       0.62         0.62        0.60
10
weighted avg    0.65         0.60        0.60
10
AUC-ROC:   0.625
LOGLOSS Value is 13.815750437193334
```

Performance Metrics for Regression Problems

We have discussed regression and its algorithms in previous chapters. Here, we are going to discuss various performance metrics that can be used to evaluate predictions for regression problems.

Mean Absolute Error (MAE)

It is the simplest error metric used in regression problems. It is basically the sum of average of the absolute difference between the predicted and actual values. In simple words, with MAE, we can get an idea of how wrong the predictions were. MAE does not indicate the direction of the model i.e. no indication about underperformance or overperformance of the model. The following is the formula to calculate MAE –

$$MAE - \frac{1}{n} \sum |Y - \hat{Y}|$$

Here, Y=Actual Output Values

And Y^^= Predicted Output Values.

We can use mean_absolute_error function of sklearn.metrics to compute MAE.

Mean Square Error (MSE)

MSE is like the MAE, but the only difference is that the it squares the difference of actual and predicted output values before summing them all instead of using the absolute value. The difference can be noticed in the following equation –

$$MSE = \frac{1}{n} \sum (Y - \hat{Y})$$

Here, Y=Actual Output Values
   And Y^^ = Predicted Output Values.
   We can use mean_squared_error function of sklearn.metrics to compute MSE.

R Squared (R2)

R Squared metric is generally used for explanatory purpose and provides an indication of the goodness or fit of a set of predicted output values to the actual output values. The following formula will help us understanding it –

$$R^2 = 1 - \frac{\frac{1}{n}\sum_{i=1}^{n}(Y_i - \hat{Y}_i)^2}{\frac{1}{n}\sum_{i=1}^{n}(Y_i - \bar{Y}_i)^2}$$

In the above equation, numerator is MSE and the denominator is the variance in Y values.

We can use r2_score function of sklearn.metrics to compute R squared value.

Example

The following is a simple recipe in Python which will give us an insight about how we can use the above explained performance metrics on regression model –

```
from sklearn.metrics import r2_score
from sklearn.metrics import mean_absolute_error
from sklearn.metrics import mean_squared_error
X_actual = [5, -1, 2, 10]
Y_predic = [3.5, -0.9, 2, 9.9]
print ('R Squared =',r2_score(X_actual, Y_predic))
print ('MAE =',mean_absolute_error(X_actual,
Y_predic))
print ('MSE =',mean_squared_error(X_actual,
Y_predic))
```

Output

```
R Squared = 0.9656060606060606
MAE = 0.42499999999999993
MSE = 0.5674999999999999
```

Automatic Workflows

In order to execute and produce results successfully, a machine learning model must automate some standard workflows. The process of automate these standard workflows can be done with the help of Scikit-learn Pipelines. From a data scientist's perspective, pipeline is a generalized, but very important concept. It basically allows data flow from its raw format to some useful information. The working of pipelines can be understood with the help of following diagram –

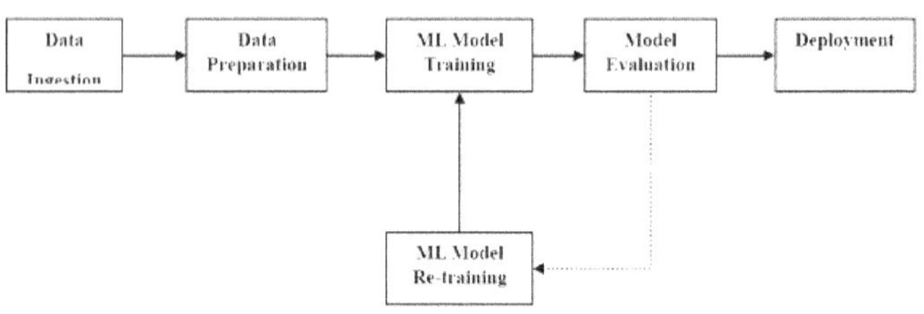

The blocks of ML pipelines are as follows –

Data ingestion – As the name suggests, it is the process of importing the data for use in ML project. The data can be extracted in real time or batches from single or multiple systems. It is one of the most challenging steps because the quality of data can affect the whole ML model.

Data Preparation – After importing the data, we need to prepare data to be used for our ML model. Data preprocessing is one of the most important technique of data preparation.

ML Model Training – Next step is to train our ML model. We have various ML algorithms like supervised, unsupervised, reinforcement to extract the features from data, and make predictions.

Model Evaluation – Next, we need to evaluate the ML model. In case of AutoML pipeline, ML model can be evaluated with the help of various statistical methods and business rules.

ML Model retraining – In case of AutoML pipeline, it is not necessary that the first model is best one. The first model is considered as a baseline model and we can train it repeatably to increase model's accuracy.

Deployment – At last, we need to deploy the model. This step involves applying and migrating the model to business operations for their use.

Challenges Accompanying ML Pipelines

In order to create ML pipelines, data scientists face many challenges. These challenges fall into the following three categories –

Quality of Data

The success of any ML model depends heavily on the quality of data. If the data we are providing to ML model is not accurate, reliable and robust, then we are going to end with wrong or misleading output.

Data Reliability

Another challenge associated with ML pipelines is the reliability of data we are providing to the ML model. As we know, there can be various sources from which data scientist can acquire data but to get the best results, it must be assured that the data sources are reliable and trusted.

Data Accessibility

To get the best results out of ML pipelines, the data itself must be accessible which requires consolidation, cleansing and curation of data. As a result of data accessibility property, metadata will be updated with new tags.

Modelling ML Pipeline and Data Preparation

Data leakage, happening from training dataset to testing dataset, is an important issue for data scientist to deal with while preparing data for ML model. Generally, at the time of data preparation, data scientist uses techniques like standardization or normalization on entire dataset before learning. But these techniques cannot help us from the leakage of data because the training dataset would have been influenced by the scale of the data in the testing dataset.

By using ML pipelines, we can prevent this data leakage because pipelines ensure that data preparation like standardization is constrained to each fold of our cross-validation procedure.

Example

The following is an example in Python that demonstrate data preparation and model evaluation workflow. For this purpose, we are using Pima Indian Diabetes dataset from Sklearn. First, we will be creating pipeline that standardized the data. Then a Linear Discriminative analysis model will be created and at last the pipeline will be evaluated using 10-fold cross validation.

First, import the required packages as follows –

```python
from pandas import read_csv
from sklearn.model_selection import KFold
from sklearn.model_selection import cross_val_score
from sklearn.preprocessing import StandardScaler
from sklearn.pipeline import Pipeline
from sklearn.discriminant_analysis import
LinearDiscriminantAnalysis
```

Now, we need to load the Pima diabetes dataset as did in previous examples –

```python
path = r"C:\pima-indians-diabetes.csv"
headernames = ['preg', 'plas', 'pres', 'skin',
```

```
'test', 'mass', 'pedi', 'age', 'class']
data = read_csv(path, names=headernames)
array = data.values
```

Next, we will create a pipeline with the help of the following code –

```
estimators = []
estimators.append(('standardize', StandardScaler()))
estimators.append(('lda',
LinearDiscriminantAnalysis()))
model = Pipeline(estimators)
```

At last, we are going to evaluate this pipeline and output its accuracy as follows –

```
kfold = KFold(n_splits=20, random_state=7)
results = cross_val_score(model, X, Y, cv=kfold)
print(results.mean())
```

Output

```
0.7790148448043184
```

The above output is the summary of accuracy of the setup on the dataset.

Modelling ML Pipeline and Feature Extraction

Data leakage can also happen at feature extraction step of ML model. That is why feature extraction procedures should also be restricted to stop data leakage in our training dataset. As in the case of data preparation, by using ML pipelines, we can prevent this data leakage also. FeatureUnion, a tool provided by ML pipelines can be used for this purpose.

Example

The following is an example in Python that demonstrates feature extraction and model evaluation workflow. For this purpose, we are using Pima Indian Diabetes dataset from Sklearn.

First, 3 features will be extracted with PCA (Principal Component Analysis). Then, 6 features will be extracted with Statistical Analysis. After feature extraction, result of multiple feature selection and extraction procedures will be combined by using

FeatureUnion tool. At last, a Logistic Regression model will be created, and the pipeline will be evaluated using 10-fold cross validation.

First, import the required packages as follows –

```
from pandas import read_csv
from sklearn.model_selection import KFold
from sklearn.model_selection import cross_val_score
from sklearn.pipeline import Pipeline
from sklearn.pipeline import FeatureUnion
from sklearn.linear_model import LogisticRegression
from sklearn.decomposition import PCA
```

```python
from sklearn.feature_selection import SelectKBest
```

Now, we need to load the Pima diabetes dataset as did in previous examples –

```python
path = r"C:\pima-indians-diabetes.csv"
headernames = ['preg', 'plas', 'pres', 'skin',
'test', 'mass', 'pedi', 'age', 'class']
data = read_csv(path, names=headernames)
array = data.values
```

Next, feature union will be created as follows –

```python
features = []
features.append(('pca', PCA(n_components=3)))
features.append(('select_best', SelectKBest(k=6)))
feature_union = FeatureUnion(features)
```

Next, pipeline will be creating with the help of following script lines –

```python
estimators = []
estimators.append(('feature_union', feature_union))
estimators.append(('logistic', LogisticRegression()))
model = Pipeline(estimators)
```

At last, we are going to evaluate this pipeline and output its accuracy as follows –

```python
kfold = KFold(n_splits=20, random_state=7)
results = cross_val_score(model, X, Y, cv=kfold)
print(results.mean())
```

Output

```
0.7789811066126855
```

The above output is the summary of accuracy of the setup on the dataset.

Improving Performance of ML Models

Performance Improvement with Ensembles

Ensembles can give us boost in the machine learning result by combining several models. Basically, ensemble models consist of several individually trained supervised learning models and their results are merged in various ways to achieve better predictive performance compared to a single model. Ensemble methods can be divided into following two groups –

Sequential ensemble methods

As the name implies, in these kind of ensemble methods, the base learners are generated sequentially. The motivation of such methods is to exploit the dependency among base learners.

Parallel ensemble methods

As the name implies, in these kind of ensemble methods, the base learners are generated in parallel. The motivation of such methods is to exploit the independence among base learners.

Ensemble Learning Methods

The following are the most popular ensemble learning methods i.e. the methods for combining the predictions from different models –

Bagging

The term bagging is also known as bootstrap aggregation. In bagging methods, ensemble model tries to improve prediction accuracy and decrease model variance by combining predictions of individual models trained over randomly generated training samples. The final prediction of ensemble model will be given by calculating the average of all predictions from the individual estimators. One of the best examples of bagging methods are random forests.

Boosting

In boosting method, the main principle of building ensemble model is to build it incrementally by training each base model estimator sequentially. As the name suggests, it basically combine several week base learners, trained sequentially over multiple iterations of training data, to build powerful ensemble. During the training of week base learners, higher weights are assigned to those learners which were misclassified earlier. The example of boosting method is AdaBoost.

Voting

In this ensemble learning model, multiple models of different types are built and some simple statistics, like calculating mean or median etc., are used to combine the predictions. This prediction will serve as the additional input for training to make the final prediction.

Bagging Ensemble Algorithms

The following are three bagging ensemble algorithms –

Bagged Decision Tree

As we know that bagging ensemble methods work well with the algorithms that have high variance and, in this concern, the best one is decision tree algorithm. In the following Python recipe, we are going to build bagged decision tree ensemble model by using BaggingClassifier function of sklearn with DecisionTreeClasifier (a classification & regression trees algorithm) on Pima Indians diabetes dataset.

First, import the required packages as follows –

```
from pandas import read_csv
from sklearn.model_selection import KFold
from sklearn.model_selection import cross_val_score
from sklearn.ensemble import BaggingClassifier
from sklearn.tree import DecisionTreeClassifier
```

Now, we need to load the Pima diabetes dataset as we did in the previous examples –

```
path = r"C:\pima-indians-diabetes.csv"
headernames = ['preg', 'plas', 'pres', 'skin',
'test', 'mass', 'pedi', 'age', 'class']
data = read_csv(path, names=headernames)
array = data.values
X = array[:,0:8]
Y = array[:,8]
```

Next, give the input for 10-fold cross validation as follows –

```
seed = 7
kfold = KFold(n_splits=10, random_state=seed)
cart = DecisionTreeClassifier()
```

We need to provide the number of trees we are going to build. Here we are building 150 trees –

```
num_trees = 150
```

Next, build the model with the help of following script –

```
model = BaggingClassifier(base_estimator=cart,
n_estimators=num_trees, random_state=seed)
```

Calculate and print the result as follows –

```
results = cross_val_score(model, X, Y, cv=kfold)
print(results.mean())
```

Output

```
0.7733766233766234
```

The output above shows that we got around 77% accuracy of our bagged decision tree classifier model.

Random Forest

It is an extension of bagged decision trees. For individual classifiers, the samples of training dataset are taken with replacement, but the trees are constructed in such a way that reduces the correlation between them. Also, a random subset of features is considered to choose each split point rather than greedily choosing the best split point in construction of each tree.

In the following Python recipe, we are going to build bagged random forest ensemble model by using RandomForestClassi fier class of sklearn on Pima Indians diabetes dataset.

First, import the required packages as follows –

```
from pandas import read_csv
from sklearn.model_selection import KFold
from sklearn.model_selection import cross_val_score
from sklearn.ensemble import RandomForestClassifier
```

Now, we need to load the Pima diabetes dataset as did in previous examples –

```
path = r"C:\pima-indians-diabetes.csv"
headernames = ['preg', 'plas', 'pres', 'skin',
```

```
'test', 'mass', 'pedi', 'age', 'class']
data = read_csv(path, names=headernames)
array = data.values
X = array[:,0:8]
Y = array[:,8]
```

Next, give the input for 10-fold cross validation as follows –

```
seed = 7
kfold = KFold(n_splits=10, random_state=seed)
```

We need to provide the number of trees we are going to build. Here we are building 150 trees with split points chosen from 5 features –

```
num_trees = 150
max_features = 5
```

Next, build the model with the help of following script –

```
model =
RandomForestClassifier(n_estimators=num_trees,
max_features=max_features)
```

Calculate and print the result as follows –

```
results = cross_val_score(model, X, Y, cv=kfold)
print(results.mean())
```

Output

```
0.7629357484620642
```

The output above shows that we got around 76% accuracy of our bagged random forest classifier model.

Extra Trees

It is another extension of bagged decision tree ensemble method. In this method, the random trees are constructed from the samples of the training dataset.

In the following Python recipe, we are going to build extra tree ensemble model by using ExtraTreesClassifier class of sklearn on Pima Indians diabetes dataset.

First, import the required packages as follows –

```
from pandas import read_csv
from sklearn.model_selection import KFold
from sklearn.model_selection import cross_val_score
from sklearn.ensemble import ExtraTreesClassifier
```

Now, we need to load the Pima diabetes dataset as did in previous examples –

```
path = r"C:\pima-indians-diabetes.csv"
headernames = ['preg', 'plas', 'pres', 'skin',
'test', 'mass', 'pedi', 'age', 'class']
data = read_csv(path, names=headernames)
array = data.values
X = array[:,0:8]
Y = array[:,8]
```

Next, give the input for 10-fold cross validation as follows –

```
seed = 7
kfold = KFold(n_splits=10, random_state=seed)
```

We need to provide the number of trees we are going to build. Here we are building 150 trees with split points chosen from 5 features –

```
num_trees = 150
max_features = 5
```

Next, build the model with the help of following script –

```
model = ExtraTreesClassifier(n_estimators=num_trees,
max_features=max_features)
```

Calculate and print the result as follows –

```
results = cross_val_score(model, X, Y, cv=kfold)
print(results.mean())
```

Output

```
0.7551435406698566
```

The output above shows that we got around 75.5% accuracy of our bagged extra trees classifier model.

Boosting Ensemble Algorithms

The followings are the two most common boosting ensemble algorithms –

AdaBoost

It is one the most successful boosting ensemble algorithm. The main key of this algorithm is in the way they give weights to the instances in dataset. Due to this the algorithm needs to pay less attention to the instances while constructing subsequent models.

In the following Python recipe, we are going to build Ada Boost ensemble model for classification by using AdaBoostClassifier class of sklearn on Pima Indians diabetes dataset.

First, import the required packages as follows –

```
from pandas import read_csv
from sklearn.model_selection import KFold
from sklearn.model_selection import cross_val_score
from sklearn.ensemble import AdaBoostClassifier
```

Now, we need to load the Pima diabetes dataset as did in previous examples –

```
path = r"C:\pima-indians-diabetes.csv"
headernames = ['preg', 'plas', 'pres', 'skin',
'test', 'mass', 'pedi', 'age', 'class']
data = read_csv(path, names=headernames)
array = data.values
```

```
X = array[:,0:8]
Y = array[:,8]
```

Next, give the input for 10-fold cross validation as follows –

```
seed = 5
kfold = KFold(n_splits=10, random_state=seed)
```

We need to provide the number of trees we are going to build. Here we are building 150 trees with split points chosen from 5 features –

```
num_trees = 50
```

Next, build the model with the help of following script –

```
model = AdaBoostClassifier(n_estimators=num_trees,
random_state=seed)
```

Calculate and print the result as follows –

```
results = cross_val_score(model, X, Y, cv=kfold)
print(results.mean())
```

Output

```
0.7539473684210527
```

The output above shows that we got around 75% accuracy of our AdaBoost classifier ensemble model.

Stochastic Gradient Boosting

It is also called Gradient Boosting Machines. In the following Python recipe, we are going to build Stochastic Gradient Boostingensemble model for classification by using GradientBoostingClassifier class of sklearn on Pima Indians diabetes dataset.

First, import the required packages as follows –

```
from pandas import read_csv
from sklearn.model_selection import KFold
from sklearn.model_selection import cross_val_score
from sklearn.ensemble import
GradientBoostingClassifier
```

Now, we need to load the Pima diabetes dataset as did in previous examples –

```
path = r"C:\pima-indians-diabetes.csv"
headernames = ['preg', 'plas', 'pres', 'skin',
'test', 'mass', 'pedi', 'age', 'class']
data = read_csv(path, names=headernames)
array = data.values
X = array[:,0:8]
Y = array[:,8]
```

Next, give the input for 10-fold cross validation as follows –

```
seed = 5
kfold = KFold(n_splits=10, random_state=seed)
```

We need to provide the number of trees we are going to build. Here we are building 150 trees with split points chosen from 5 features –

```
num_trees = 50
```

Next, build the model with the help of following script –

```
model =
GradientBoostingClassifier(n_estimators=num_trees,
random_state=seed)
```

Calculate and print the result as follows –

```
results = cross_val_score(model, X, Y, cv=kfold)
print(results.mean())
```

Output

```
0.77465582365003418
```

The output above shows that we got around 77.5% accuracy of our Gradient Boosting classifier ensemble model.

Voting Ensemble Algorithms

As discussed, voting first creates two or more standalone models from training dataset and then a voting classifier will wrap the model along with taking the average of the predictions of sub-model whenever needed new data.

In the following Python recipe, we are going to build Voting ensemble model for classification by using VotingClassifier class of sklearn on Pima Indians diabetes dataset. We are combining the predictions of logistic regression, Decision Tree classifier and SVM together for a classification problem as follows –

First, import the required packages as follows –

```
from pandas import read_csv
from sklearn.model_selection import KFold
from sklearn.model_selection import cross_val_score
from sklearn.linear_model import LogisticRegression
from sklearn.tree import DecisionTreeClassifier
from sklearn.svm import SVC
from sklearn.ensemble import VotingClassifier
```

Now, we need to load the Pima diabetes dataset as did in previous examples –

```
path = r"C:\pima-indians-diabetes.csv"
headernames = ['preg', 'plas', 'pres', 'skin',
'test', 'mass', 'pedi', 'age', 'class']
data = read_csv(path, names=headernames)
array = data.values
X = array[:,0:8]
Y = array[:,8]
```

Next, give the input for 10-fold cross validation as follows –

```
kfold = KFold(n_splits=10, random_state=7)
```

Next, we need to create sub-models as follows –

```python
estimators = []
model1 = LogisticRegression()
estimators.append(('logistic', model1))
model2 = DecisionTreeClassifier()
estimators.append(('cart', model2))
model3 = SVC()
estimators.append(('svm', model3))
```

Now, create the voting ensemble model by combining the predictions of above created sub models.

```python
ensemble = VotingClassifier(estimators)
results = cross_val_score(ensemble, X, Y, cv=kfold)
print(results.mean())
```

Output

```
0.7382262474367738
```

The output above shows that we got around 74% accuracy of our voting classifier ensemble model.

References

Python Basics:

1. Beazley, D. M. (2009) – Python Essential Reference.
2. McKinney, W. (2017) – Python for Data Analysis.
3. VanderPlas, J. (2016) – Python Data Science Handbook.

Data Science Fundamentals:

1. Grolemund, H., & Wickham, H. (2017) – "R for Data Science.
2. Provost, F., & Fawcett, T. (2013) – Data Science for Business.

Machine Learning:

1. Hastie, T., Tibshirani, R., & Friedman, J. (2009) – The Elements of Statistical Learning.
2. Raschka, S., & Mirjalili, V. (2019) – Python Machine Learning.

Deep Learning:

1. Goodfellow, I., Bengio, Y., & Courville, A. (2016) – Deep Learning.

2. Chollet, F. (2017) – Deep Learning with Python.

Data Visualization:

1. Tufte, E. R. (2001) – The Visual Display of Quantitative Information.
2. Cairo, A. (2016) – The Truthful Art: Data, Charts, and Maps for Communication.

Python Libraries:

1. Pedregosa, F., et al. (2011) – Scikit learn: Machine Learning in Python.
2. McKinney, W. (2018) – Python for Data Science For Dummies.

Case Studies and Applications:

1. O'Neil, C., & Schutt, R. (2013) – Doing Data Science.
2. Provost, F., & Fawcett, T. (2013) – Data Science for Business.

Ethics in Data Science:

1. O'Neil, C. (2016) – Weapons of Math Destruction: How Big Data Increases Inequality and Threatens Democracy.
2. Diakopoulos, N. (2016) – Automating the News: How Algorithms Are Rewriting the Media.